Apostolic Purity

In Pursuit of His Excellence
Sequel to Five Pillars of The Apostolic

Dr. Michael Scantlebury

Foreword by
Apostle John Eckhardt

Preface by
Dr. Kelley Varner

Dr. Scantlebury has taken a*uthor's prerogative* in capitalizing certain words that are not usually capitalized according to standard grammatical practice. The references to apostles and purity are capitalized and bolded many times to give greater emphasis to the main theme of this book. Also, please note that the name satan and related names are not capitalized as we choose not to acknowledge him, even to the point of disregarding standard grammatical practice.

Hebrew and Greek definitions are taken from James Strong, *Strong's Exhaustive Concordance of the Bible* (Peabody, MA: Hendrickson Publishers, n.d.).

Apostolic Purity
ISBN 1-894928-11-3
© Copyright 2003 by Michael Scantlebury

Cover design by: Word Alive Press Inc.
Printed by: Word Alive Press Inc.

Editorial Consultant: Amrita Bastians

Dedication

I dedicate this book to all the true end-time Apostles that the Lord Jesus Christ is raising up by His Holy Spirit - To those who will not compromise, or prostitute the calling and anointing. I also dedicate it to those who have fearlessly stood for the cause of the gospel of the Kingdom at the cost of their lives. To Pastor Ajith Abeyratne of Sri Lanka who has been standing firm in God through extreme odds – with a true show of Apostolic Grace upon him.

And once again I am truly grateful to the *Apostle and High Priest of my confession, Christ Jesus* for granting me the Grace to write another book.

Acknowledgements

I would like to take this opportunity to thank Dr. Noel Woodroffe for the clear and excellent teaching I received on the Elijah spirit as I sat under his tutelage in Elijah Centre.

I would also like to thank our administrative assistant Amrita Bastians for her tireless and unending support as she spent many hours editing and critiquing the manuscript of this book.

To Dr. Kelley Varner and Apostle John Eckhardt who graciously took the time from their busy schedules to read and foreword this book.

Table of Contents

Foreword

Preface

Commendations 7

Introduction 19

Chapter 1: The Return Of The Elijah Spirit 25
John's Ministry 27
Further Clarity 32
The Spirit And Power Of Elijah 36
Pitfalls Of The Elijah Spirit 43
Understanding The Spirit Of Jezebel 47

Chapter 2: Defeating The Spirit Of Jezebel 53
Let Us Focus On Jehu's Anointing 55
The Need For The Apostolic And Prophetic To Destroy 62
The Jezebel Spirit

Chapter 3: Working A Work In Our Time 69
Unbelief 70
The Apostolic Commissioning And Sending Of Joshua 76
Change Is Constant 78
His Vineyard 79
Wine 80
Lame Excuses 88
Wineskins – Carriers Of The Anointing 93

Chapter 4: Purification For Possessing 95
The Ark Of The Covenant 98
Issues Of The Contents Of The Ark 100
There Must Be A Readiness To Hear The Word Of 108
The Lord
The Twelve Stone Principle 108

Gilgal   109
The "So That" Principle   114

Chapter 5: Kings And Priests   117
The Kingly-Priesthood Of The Believer   117
A Brief Note On Melchizedek   119
The Royal Priesthood   123

Chapter 6: Part I - Qualifications And   127
Blemishes Of The Priesthood I
Merchandizing Of The Anointing And Gifting   130
Reviewing The Zadok Anointing   139

Chapter 6: Part II - Qualifications And   159
Blemishes Of The Priesthood II
Blindness   164
Lameness   168
Flat Nose   172
Deformed Or Superfluous   174
Broken Foot   175
Broken Hand   176

Chapter 6: Part III - Qualifications And   179
Blemishes Of The Priesthood III
Hunch-Backed   179
The Dwarf   180
Blemish In The Eye   181
Scurvy – Eczema Or Skin Disease   183
Scabs   186
Broken Stones   190

Appendix - Apostolic Definition/Reference In
Scripture

Other Titles By The Author

Recommended Titles By Other Authors

Foreword

The apostolic movement is the fastest growing movement in the worldwide church today. There are more books being written on the subject of the apostolic ministry than at any other time in history. There are many leaders who are interested in apostolic ministry and desire to walk in it correctly and accurately. This book will bring balance to those who are seeking the truth concerning apostles and apostolic ministry.

These are apostolic times and we should believe God for apostolic results. Many are claiming apostleship and new apostolic networks are arising continuously. I am a proponent of the current restoration of apostolic ministry and desire to see it restored fully and correctly. As an advocate for emerging apostles, I am always interested and look forward to new insight and revelation in this area. This is why I recommend this book.

It is important for us to test those who claim apostleship. We are admonished to prove all things. All ministries must have the character of the Lord. We must reject any ministry that does not measure up to the purity and character of apostles and apostolic ministry found in the scriptures. This book will help believers to judge properly the many ministries that are presently claiming to have been sent from God.

Purity is defined as the condition or quality of being pure. It also means freedom from anything that debases, contaminates, or pollutes. The enemy always tries to pervert and corrupt what God is restoring. The devil hates and fears apostolic ministry and will do everything in his power to weaken and defile it. The apostolic ministry must be characterized by purity. The church must be challenged to have ministry that is pure and uncorrupted.

Michael Scantlebury has a heart to see the apostolic ministry restored correctly. He has seen the abuses that this kind of ministry can bring. His desire is to warn the church and teach the believer properly concerning this present wave of restoration. Without purity the apostolic ministry can become a dangerous wave that brings more hurt than blessing.

The church must be challenged to receive the apostolic ministry. We must contend for the faith that was once delivered to the saints (Jude 3). To contend means to fight for or wrestle for. Many are contending for the apostolic ministry in its fullness. We don't desire to settle for anything less than the fullness of what is found in the word of God. Allow this book to minister to you and help you receive what God is doing in its fullness and purity.

If we are to walk correctly in what God is doing today we must have pure hearts and pure motives. Any other motive will cause us to abuse the authority God has given us. Without purity we will not be able to handle the tremendous amount of authority and power that is being released today through the apostolic ministry. God has entrusted us with His power, and we must be good stewards of what we have received.

As you consider what is said, the Lord will give you understanding in all things (2 Timothy 2:7). Consider the message of this book. This is important truth that must be adhered to by those interested in apostolic ministry. We must live by the words from scripture if we are to prosper in this current restoration. God will bless us as we keep our hearts and motives pure.

Apostle John Eckhardt
Leader of Crusaders Ministry
Apostolic Leader of I.M.P.A.C.T Network
Chicago, Illinois, USA

Preface

These are unprecedented days of restoration and reformation. God now raises up a company of men and women articulating "one sound," one voice (2 Chronicles 5:13), heralding the glory of the Lord that is about to fill the earth. Dr. Michael Scantlebury of Dominion-Life International Ministries, Vancouver, Canada, is such a voice.

The work before you, "Apostolic Purity – In Pursuit of His Excellence," is a compendium of "present truth" (2 Peter 1:12), setting forth many truths that the Holy Spirit is presently making real to the Church throughout the nations.

The last chapter of Malachi and the story of the transfiguration narrated in Matthew chapter 17 reveal that the "Elijah spirit" of ministry, turning the hearts of the fathers (apostles) toward the sons, and the hearts of the sons toward the fathers, highlights the present apostolic reformation. Our brother clearly sets this forth in Chapters One and Two of this writing.

Chapter Three underscores the ministry of Joshua, the one who causes others to inherit. It continues to unfold apostolic purity with regard to the wine and the wineskins. Too many of God's people want the blessing without the procedure. There is an ordering and a processing of the people of God in these days.

His next chapter moves us deeper into the apostolic

restoration, highlighting the Ark of the Covenant, followed by his unique presentation of two key principles—the Twelve Stone Principle and the "So That" Principle.

Chapters Five and Six close this treatise by noting that our pursuit of excellence is our pursuit of HIM! The "more excellent ministry" of our Lord Jesus Christ after the order of Melchizedek (Hebrews 5:1-8:6) is the "royal priesthood" of 1 Peter 2:9—we are "kings and priests" (Revelation 1:6; 5:10). The practical paradigm of this end-time truth is then made clear by unfolding the qualifications of the priesthood.

The message before you is powerful, clean, and clear— it keenly demonstrates "Apostolic Purity." May you be blessed to read it as I was. Our brother has set a full table. Enjoy! Then go forth!

Dr. Kelley Varner
Apostle, Praise Tabernacle Ministries
Richlands, North Carolina, USA

Commendations

Dr. Roger W. Sapp, All Nations Ministries, Texas, USA

"Michael Scantlebury has once again given us opportunity to consider the ministry of the modern apostle. In his book *Apostolic Purity*, he has revealed how the apostolic ministry coming forth today will lead to the Church's final destiny to be holy and Christ-like when Her Saviour Jesus Christ comes. Throughout this book, Scantlebury shines the bright light of apostolic New Testament revelation on the hidden truths found in Old Testament shadows. By doing this, he captures readers with the importance of holiness to the end-time plan of God."

Apostle Bret A. Wade, Global Impact Church, Huntsville, Alabama, USA

"Excellent! Elder Michael Scantlebury does justice to the present move of the Spirit that is especially among His leaders. It is imperative that we are pure in our intents and motives. It's a move that is fought and ignored by some, yet stands out as the foundation for success in the future of apostolic & prophetic ministries. I have thoroughly enjoyed reading "Apostolic Purity". It is a clear reflection of the biblical requirement and expectation of purity. The process of change is simply and clearly defined.

I highly recommend this book to all leaders, ministers and saints for a proper prophetic perspective on how to respond to the Lord in this hour of destiny. "Apostolic Purity" will cause us to go on to new levels in Christ as we progress in His kingdom. Let us possess with pure hearts!"

Dr. Bill Smith, Apostle, Christ as Life Christian Centre, McKinney, Texas, USA

"Michael Scantlebury has captured the heart of the Lord concerning the life and ministry of the apostle. The Lord Jesus has blessed the Church with many apostles and they are in all stages of growth. I highly recommend this book be in the hands of the five-fold ministry. It is a book that should be taught in every Bible School. Righteousness and Holy living is the door to the apostolic ministry."

M. Adrienne Hawthorne, Founder, (Now residing in heaven) The Rochester Apostolic and Prophetic Alliance, Rochester, NY USA

"As we listen to the voices in different streams, we hear much discussion regarding the restoration of the apostle and the apostolic ministry. Elder Scantlebury, in *Apostolic Purity*, helps us to understand the present ministry of the apostle through a discussion apostolic grace, focusing on Gods' standards of holiness, purity, and righteousness. In a scholarly and prophetic treatment Scripture, Elder Scantlebury challenges us to a time of self-inspection as we continue to press into the purposes and the timing of God. As we minister to the Lord and His Church, He calls us to fight in the intensity of the battle! I highly recommend Apostolic Purity for those who desire to understand and respond to God's call to character over gifting."

Pastor Ernest Culley, Agape Life Centre, Vancouver, B.C., Canada

"Pastor Scantlebury has provided a valuable resource in Apostolic Purity, urging the Body of Christ into greater heights of holiness with God. His evident passion and the teachings provided will move us further down the road to embrace the excellence of Jesus. Read and be blessed."

Apostle Sam A. Webb, Grace Bible Ministries International, Hawaii, USA

"Michael has written concerning his passion for the full restoration of the apostle. His passion has come to new levels as he speaks with great conviction about the transition that is happening in the Body of Christ. He voices the cry of the Spirit for the true and pure expression of that ministry. I encourage you to read this book and capture the same passion as we all move closer to our Lord's purposes in the earth."

Pastor Jana Alcorn, Founder and Senior Pastor of Harvest Church in Albertville, Alabama, USA

"Apostolic Purity represents a trumpet call from the Holy Spirit to all who have a hearing ear in these triumphant days. Michael Scantlebury's apostolic revelation transports the reader from comfort to confrontation, satisfaction to searching, and from passiveness to purity. This book will not leave you in the waiting room, but will transfer the reader directly into Divine surgery. Allow the skilful Hand of the Lord to bring wholeness as you embark on the journey into Apostolic Purity."

Gideon Chiu, Senior Pastor, Church Of Zion, Richmond BC, Canada

"Our Lord Jesus commended the church at Ephesus "for testing those who claim to be apostles but are not" (Revelation 2:2). In *Apostolic Purity*, Michael Scantlebury sets forth an "apostolic plumb line" for this ministry that God is surely restoring in our day. I believe the prophetic insights of the book will help pave the way for the restoration of the true apostles before our Lord's return."

Pastor Daniel Farina, Christian Assembly, Grand Island, New York, USA

"The title of the Book by my friend and comrade, Michael Scantlebury, is quite appropriate, for the writer has sought for Apostolic Purity in his own life and ministry. Having been in the presence of this humble servant, I have heard and seen a large measure of purity seep out of his life-style and ministry. In fact, in one of the illustrations that Michael uses in this volume, the Image of the Refiner is clearly seen in his walk with the Lord.

Having read other writings by this same author, I fully recommend them as required reading for Pastors, young and old, as well as interested believers who love to know what God is saying and doing in this season. The continued use of Scripture reference always brings one back to the Foundation of our Faith...The precious Word of God. Brother Michael's ability to compare Scripture with Scripture makes this a volume that fills ones heart as well as ones mind with the Voice of God.

It's challenging reading! And reading that takes you right into the presence of God. The call to purity is clearly sounded! The question is: "Is it being heard?" This is one volume that tells it directly so that unmistakably one can posture himself into a position to become pure and powerful for God."

Read it! It will change and challenge you!

Symon Boschma, Minister and Author, Everson, Washington, USA

"In "Apostolic Purity," Elder Michael Scantlebury writes with passion about the restoration of the powerful ministry gift of the apostle to Christ's end-time Church. The author, a man who follows the leading of the Holy Spirit, shares intriguing revelations on this subject that are seasoned with words of caution; exhorting mature believers to wisely deal with those who claim to be apostles but are not. This book, rich with God's Word, also contains keen insights and understanding on the qualifications and blemishes of the priesthood that will be relevant to every believer seeking greater service in His kingdom."

Doug Fortune, Minister and Author, Trumpet Call Apostolic/Prophetic Ministry

"As I read through Michael Scantlebury's book *Apostolic Purity*, I realized that Michael's message is a *Voice* worth heeding. Just as in Revelation 1:12 where John turned from his present position to see the *Voice*; Michael calls us to turn from our present inaccurate positions to see the *Voice* of the apostolic. *Apostolic Purity* is challenging and encouraging, biblically accurate and a message for this hour."

Apostolic Purity
Introduction

In every dispensation, in every move of God's Holy Spirit to bring restoration and reformation to His Church, righteousness, holiness and purity has always been of utmost importance to the Lord. And it is no different in the current move of God that is bringing apostolic restoration to His Church.

These are the end-times and we are in a mighty move of God. These are the best days to accomplish the Will of the Lord. There is a change of leadership taking place as the Lord establishes the *"new order"* that would take us deeper into the 21st century and beyond.

God has released the *"keys to the Kingdom"*, and there are all kinds of dimensions being opened up in the spirit:

"And I will give you the *keys of the kingdom* of heaven, and whatever you bind on earth will be bound in heaven, and whatever you loose on earth will be loosed in heaven." Matthew 16:19 (Italics added)

There is wisdom being released for us to know which key opens which realm as the scripture clearly says that Jesus gave keys (plural).

The realm that is being opened up at this time is the "apostolic" the master key to which is a *"higher level of purity"*.

There is a dimension to the *"baptism of fire"* that God is releasing to purify His people in this hour:

"I indeed baptize you with water unto repentance, but He who is coming after me is mightier than I, whose sandals I am not worthy to carry, He will baptize you with the Holy Spirit *and fire*. His winnowing fan is in His hand, and He will thoroughly clean out His threshing floor, and gather His wheat into the barn; but He will burn up the chaff with unquenchable fire." Matthew 3:11-12 (Italics added)

"He will *sit as a refiner and a purifier* of silver; He will *purify* the sons of Levi, And *purge* them as gold and silver, That *they may offer to the LORD An offering in righteousness*." Malachi 3:3 (Italics added)

"Behold what manner of love the Father has bestowed on us, that we should be called children of God! Therefore the world does not know us, because it did not know Him. Beloved, now we are children of God; and it has not yet been revealed what we shall be, but we know that when He is revealed, we shall be like Him, for we shall see Him as He is. And everyone who has this hope in Him *purifies himself, just as He is pure.*" 1 John 3:1-3 (Italics added)

"But we all, with unveiled face, beholding as in a mirror the glory of the Lord, *are being transformed into the same image from glory to glory*, just as by the Spirit of the Lord." 2 Corinthians 3:18 (Italics added)

In many places, the people of God are crying out for His Manifested Presence.   Fed-up with mere programs, activities and shallow religious works, Spirit-Filled, Saints of God from every nation are storming heaven and proclaiming that "the knowledge of the *Glory of God* must cover the earth, as the waters cover the sea."   God is about to respond, but it will be as in the book of Malachi:

"Behold, I send My messenger, and he will prepare the way before Me.   And *the Lord, whom you seek, will suddenly come* to His temple, even the Messenger of the covenant, in whom you delight.   Behold, He is coming, says the Lord of hosts.   But who can endure the day of His coming?   And who can stand when He appears?   For He is like a *refiner's fire* and like launderers' soap. He will sit as a *refiner and a purifier of silver; He will purify the sons of Levi*, and *purge them as gold and silver,* that they may offer to the Lord an offering in righteousness."   Malachi 3:1-3 (Italics added)

There is a purifying that has already begun in the ranks of professing Christianity.   Some apostles in training are being cast into the backsides of the desert to be purified. Others are being purified in motion, they are in charge of networks and ministries, but there is a deep inner work being done. Still, others are being purified under the *Saul and Laban types of ministries* – Saul took the best from the people and Laban deceived Jacob into working longer for him before receiving his legitimate inheritance. However, the Father chooses to do it, it is being done, so that the earth can see His Glory through the Church.

The word refine is the Hebrew word "tsaraph"; and is rendered - to melt; refine; test or purify, with regards to metals - it also carries the idea of any kind of refining, whether literal or figurative. It also refers to the melting process whereby impurities are removed from precious metals, such as gold and silver.

In fact I understand that in ancient days the refiner would sit before the crucible, fixing his eye on the metal. He would do this to ensure that the heat was not too intense that it would destroy the metal, but that it remained in the fire at the right degree of heat, for the exact period of time.

The refiner knew exactly when the silver was ready, and that was when he saw his own image reflected in the glowing mass. At that precise moment he knew the dross was completely removed, and his task was accomplished.

In like manner, our heavenly Refiner is sitting as our purifier, waiting to see His Image reflected in us:

"But He knows the way that I take; When He has tested me, I shall come forth as gold." Job 23:10

"The refining pot is for silver and the furnace for gold, But the LORD tests the hearts." Proverbs 17:3

"Behold, I have refined you, but not as silver; I have tested you in the furnace of affliction." Isaiah 48:10

"For they indeed for a few days chastened us as seemed best to them, but He for our profit, that we may be partakers of His holiness. Now no chastening seems to be joyful for the present, but painful; nevertheless, afterward it yields the peaceable fruit of righteousness to those who have been trained by it." Hebrews 12:10-11

Another meticulous example of this level of purifying and perfecting of His people can be found in the example of the potter and the clay.

As we review the ancient art of making earthenware vessels, we see that potters would place their earthenware vessels into ovens to temper, similar to what is done today. However, with one major difference as they did not have sophisticated timepieces and technological equipment, as we do today; their method of knowing when the vessel was ready differs from ours, and has great spiritual relevance to us today.

The potter knew that some pieces of his work, according to its design and shape could take a longer or shorter time in the furnace. So you may ask, if they had no equipment how did he know when his work of art was ready? The vessel *"sang"* or made a distinct noise!

Yes, *sang*. The potter would rely on the sound that emerged from the piece of pottery at the precise moment it was ready to be taken out.   The potter would say, "It is time … it is singing".

This is similar to the way the Lord deals with us at times as we go through what is called the furnace. He will not remove us until we sing. We all need to "sing" when we are going through our furnace of affliction. Remember that scripture in Isaiah 48:10 where the Lord says "I have tested you in the furnace of affliction."

Remember that God does not bring pain or misfortune to our lives, but He will most definitely work through them to perfect us. As the apostolic comes forth, the Lord will be listening for a certain "*sound*" that will signal the time of its maturity.

Dr. Michael Scantlebury
Dominion-Life International Ministries
Vancouver, BC, Canada

Chapter 1
The Return Of The Elijah Spirit

In the book of **Malachi**, which was the last documented speaking of God until the birth of Jesus over four hundred years later, we see Him placing great emphasis on *purity and righteousness.* All this cleansing was to take place before the coming of Jesus and it was two fold in nature. While we know that John the Baptist fulfilled the role of being the forerunner to Jesus (*for he came in the spirit and power of Elijah*), we also know that there is a dimension to the fulfillment of that prophetic word which is still to come.

The following passages of scripture will assist in bringing greater clarity to this. First we read:

"Now after six days Jesus took Peter, James, and John his brother, led them up on a high mountain by themselves; and He was transfigured before them. His face shone like the sun, and His clothes became as white as the light. And behold, Moses and *Elijah appeared to them, talking with Him.* Then Peter answered and said to Jesus, "Lord, it is good for us to be here; if You wish, let us make here three tabernacles: one for You, one for Moses, and one for *Elijah.*" While he was still speaking, behold, a bright cloud overshadowed them; and suddenly a voice came out of the cloud, saying, "This is My beloved Son, in whom I am well pleased. Hear Him!" And when the disciples heard it, they fell on their faces and were greatly afraid. But Jesus came and touched them and said, "Arise, and do not be afraid." When they had lifted up their eyes, they saw no one but Jesus only. Now as they came down from the mountain, Jesus commanded them, saying, "Tell the vision to no one until the Son of Man is risen from the dead." *And His disciples asked Him, saying, "Why then do the scribes say that Elijah must come first?" Jesus answered and said to them, "Indeed, Elijah is coming first and will restore all things. But I say to you that Elijah has come already,* and they did not know him but did to him whatever they wished. Likewise the Son of Man is also about to suffer at their hands." Then the disciples understood that He spoke to them of John the Baptist." Matthew 17:1-13 (Italics added)

In the preceding text we read some very important statements by Jesus, especially verses 11-13 when He declared that *Elijah is coming!*

Next we read:

"Now *this is the testimony of John*, when the Jews sent priests and Levites from Jerusalem to ask him, "Who are you?"   He confessed, and did not deny, but confessed, "I am not the Christ." *And they asked him, "What then? Are you Elijah?" He said, "I am not."* "Are you the Prophet?" And he answered, "No."   Then they said to him, "Who are you, that we may give an answer to those who sent us? What do you say about yourself?" He said: "I am 'The voice of one crying in the wilderness: "Make straight the way of the LORD, "as the Prophet Isaiah said."   Now those who were sent were from the Pharisees. And they asked him, saying, "Why then do you baptize if you are not the Christ, nor Elijah, nor the Prophet?" John answered them, saying, "I baptize with water, but there stands One among you whom you do not know. It is He who, coming after me, is preferred before me, whose sandal strap I am not worthy to loose." These things were done in Bethabara beyond the Jordan, where John was baptizing."   John 1:19-28 (Italics added)

Here we note the accurate testimony of John concerning himself as he made some very pertinent statements and declared – that *he was not Elijah*!

John's Ministry

"But the angel said to him, "Do not be afraid, Zacharias, for your prayer is heard; and your wife Elizabeth will bear you a son, and you shall call his name John. And you will have joy and gladness, and *many will rejoice at his birth.* For he will be great in the sight of the Lord, *and shall drink neither wine nor strong drink. He will also be filled with the Holy Spirit,* even from his mother's womb. And *he will turn many of the children of Israel to the Lord their God. He will also go before Him in the spirit and power of Elijah,* 'to turn the hearts of the fathers to the children,' and the disobedient to the wisdom of the just, *to make ready a people prepared for the Lord."* Luke 1:13-17 (Italics added)

"When the messengers of John had departed, He began to speak to the multitudes concerning John: "What did you go out into the wilderness to see? A reed shaken by the wind? But what did you go out to see? A man clothed in soft garments? Indeed those who are gorgeously apparelled and live in luxury are in kings' courts. *But what did you go out to see? A Prophet? Yes, I say to you, and more than a Prophet.* This is he of whom it is written: 'Behold, I send My messenger before Your face, who will prepare Your way before You.'" Luke 7:24-27 (Italics added)

As we press further into the purposes of the Lord, I would like us to re-visit the ministry of John the Baptist, as this is most relevant to the times in which we live.

To fully understand our ministry in these last days, it is imperative that we understand the ministry of John as he functioned in a similar role to us, the endtime church. Most people have come to accept John as a prophet who walked and functioned in the "spirit and power of Elijah" and this is partly true. However, as Jesus spoke about John before his death, *Jesus declared that John was more* (not better) than a prophet. I submit to you that Jesus was speaking about an apostolic dimension operating in John's life. The Church of Jesus Christ is built upon the foundation of the apostles and prophets with Jesus Christ being the Chief Cornerstone. The apostolic and prophetic was and still is an inseparable ministry in the Church of Jesus Christ.

Malachi prophesied of the coming of Elijah the Prophet before the second coming of Jesus. However, there is a two-fold fulfillment to this prophetic word. John the Baptist fulfilled the first, and the endtime Church is fulfilling the second.

The prophetic anointing releases the ability to see events in the future and to foretell them. The apostolic anointing has the ability to bring to pass what the prophetic sees. The apostolic anointing says, [1]"This is that which was spoken by the prophets"

Let us briefly look at five things the apostolic\prophetic anointing caused that was resident in John the Baptist that is valuable to us as we continue preparing the way for the move of God in this region and in the nations of the earth.

- **Many will rejoice at his birth**
  John's [2]birth caused many to rejoice because he signalled a new mentality to kingdom activity, which

---

[1] Acts 2:16
[2] Luke 1:14

was [3]kingdom violence. He was able to bring forth the *manifestation* of the [4]words prophesied by the law and the prophets. He also brought joy to many because he declared the Messiah to them.

- **He did not drink wine nor strong drink**
Wine is a mocker of the true anointing and strong drink causes us to forget the law – which is *self-government*! [5]John was truly a man of internal self-government and that caused him to be intensely focused. This is a reflection of the [6]Nazirite vow, which was accompanied by the fact that no razor was to come upon the head. Hair represents authority, and hair being cut was a sign of one's authority being severed. Ergo, this apostolic\prophetic anointing that is being released today will move us into a stronger place of self-government and authority in the things of the Spirit.

- **Filled with the Spirit of the Lord**
[7]This is powerful, as it is a higher dimension than that of earthly fathering or mentoring. This is the realm of divine impartation, fathering and release. John's father, Zacharias, could not father or mentor him in order to release him into what God had ordained for him to accomplish - (Zacharias was in unbelief and functioned under an old order which was about to change with the ministry of his son John). Therefore God Himself, had to mentor and train John. This is what gave him the

---

[3] Matthew 11:12
[4] Matthew 11:13
[5] Luke 1:15
[6] Numbers 6:1-8
[7] Luke 1:15

power and anointing to function the way he did and released him to be able to identify the Christ – Our Saviour and Lord!   There is a dimension of the revelation of Christ that the Lord is bringing forth through the apostolic\prophetic that is designed to turn many to the Lord.   There is going to be a new release in the evangelistic realm because of the release of this apostolic\prophetic anointing.

- **The power to turn the hearts of fathers, children and the disobedient**[8]
An awesome anointing for impartation and wisdom is released through this apostolic\prophetic anointing. There is also the ability to release true fatherhood from a position of strength and purity.   The spirit of impartation and wisdom is also very active in this anointing.

- **To make a people prepared for the Lord**[9]
There is a finishing anointing that is also released through this apostolic\prophetic anointing that is being released in this hour. The final product will be a people who are absolutely ready for the return of the Lord.

Remember Malachi prophesied that before the second coming of Jesus that the spirit of Elijah would return. Some may want to argue that Malachi prophesied about John the Baptist.   However, as we said before Malachi's prophesy is two-fold.   Elijah *has come* and Elijah *is to*

---

[8] Luke 1:17
[9] Luke 1:17

come! If we look closer at the actual time that Malachi's prophetic word was to be accomplished, we would see that he places its fulfillment at the end of the age, before the second return of Jesus. We read in Malachi 4:5 "Behold, I will send you Elijah the Prophet *Before the coming of the great and dreadful day of the Lord.*" (Italics added) This had to be referring to the second coming of Jesus because His first coming was not a great and dreadful day. It was a day of deliverance and salvation.

Further Clarity

An amazing event took place in the life of Jesus that will bring absolute clarity to this prophetic word and the relevance it has to the current move of God.

Jesus was about to begin His earthly ministry and after His cousin John baptized Him, was led away into the wilderness to be tested by the devil. After forty days and nights of rigorous prayer and fasting, He defeats the devil and immediately steps into His public ministry. He went to Galilee and the surrounding cities and preached. Evidently, He was well received in those regions[10].

After His ministry in those regions He returned to Nazareth, His hometown, and as was His custom He went into the synagogue and stood up to read and was handed the book of the prophet Isaiah and He read:

"The Spirit of the LORD is upon Me, Because He has anointed Me To preach the gospel to the poor; He has

---

[10] Luke 4:13-15

sent Me to heal the brokenhearted, To proclaim liberty to the captives And recovery of sight to the blind, To set at liberty those who are oppressed; To proclaim the acceptable year of the LORD." Then He closed the book, and gave it back to the attendant and sat down. And the eyes of all who were in the synagogue were fixed on Him. And He began to say to them, "Today *this Scripture is fulfilled* in your hearing." Luke 4:18-22 (Italics added)

What an incredible moment that must have been, all eyes were fixed on Jesus as He read and then made that proclamation. I mean this is the hometown boy. Not only that, but news traveled fast even in those days (without all the amenities of modern science, World Wide Web included) of His exploits in the surrounded cities, especially Capernaum.

However, let us take a closer look at the text of scripture that Jesus quoted from, and see the incredible implications of His actions. Jesus was quoting from the book of Isaiah:

"The Spirit of the Lord GOD is upon Me, Because the LORD has anointed Me To preach good tidings to the poor; He has sent Me to heal the brokenhearted, To proclaim liberty to the captives, And the opening of the prison to those who are bound; To proclaim the acceptable year of the LORD, *And the day of vengeance of our God...*" Isaiah 61:1-2 (Italics added)

As can be noticed, Jesus ends His reading right in the middle of a sentence. Well, what is the implication of this, one may ask?

The Implication Is!

Jesus' first entrance upon planet earth was not to bring judgment, but *Salvation* (for that's what His name meant – Matthew 1:21: "And she will bring forth a Son, and you shall call His name Jesus, for He will save His people from their sins."). This is why He stopped His apostolic decree right in the middle of the sentence. This takes us even further into another line of questioning - who will proclaim *the day of vengeance of our God?* The answer can only be – *We the Church – Jesus' Body!*

In the light of this we can now see and understand that Malachi was truly speaking about the days preceding the second advent of Jesus. When He comes the second time He will not be coming to save the people from their sins, but He will come as *King and Judge!*

Preparing The Way

As it was with Jesus' first coming so shall it be with His second. John the Baptist preceded Him, walking in the spirit and power of Elijah "preparing the way" before Him:

"In those days John the Baptist came preaching in the wilderness of Judea, and saying, "Repent, for the kingdom of heaven is at hand!" For this is he who was spoken of by the Prophet Isaiah, saying: "The voice of one crying in the wilderness: *'Prepare the way of the LORD; Make His paths straight.'*" Matthew 3:1-3 (Italics added)

Just before his birth, the Angel of the Lord appeared to

his father Zacharias and proclaimed:

> "Then an angel of the Lord appeared to him, standing on the right side of the altar of incense. And when Zacharias saw him, he was troubled, and fear fell upon him. But the angel said to him, "Do not be afraid, Zacharias, for your prayer is heard; and your wife Elizabeth will bear you a son, and you shall call his name John. And you will have joy and gladness, and many will rejoice at his birth. For he will be great in the sight of the Lord, and shall drink neither wine nor strong drink. He will also be filled with the Holy Spirit, even from his mother's womb. And he will turn many of the children of Israel to the Lord their God. *He will also go before Him in the spirit and power of Elijah, 'to turn the hearts of the fathers to the children,' and the disobedient to the wisdom of the just, to make ready a people prepared for the Lord."* Luke 1:11-17 (Italics added)

In like manner there must be a people in this hour who can and must *"prepare the way"* for the Second Coming of Jesus.

They must also walk *in the spirit and power of Elijah, to turn the hearts of the fathers to the children, and the disobedient to the wisdom of the just, to make ready a people prepared for the Lord.* If you can receive it I submit to you that the [11]apostolic/prophetic restoration that is now taking place in the Body of Christ is being released

---

[11] You can read the author's book "Five Pillars of The Apostolic" for a more in-depth analysis on the restorations of Apostles.

in the same spirit and power of Elijah. There is such an awesome anointing being released into the Body of Christ for uncompromising function in the will of God. In every nation, in every jurisdiction, men and women of God are beginning to forsake the error of their ways, repenting and renouncing sinful practices and crying out for the move of God's Spirit as never before. I tell you, God has already begun to respond, and "*purity*" is the buzzword in the spirit realm and in the heart of all of God's true apostles!

The Spirit And Power Of Elijah!

To fully understand this we must return to the life of Elijah and re-visit Mt. Carmel[12].

As we read the life of this great man of God we realize that everything that happened in his life was training for his Mt. Carmel experience. God raised him up to change an apostate nation by aggressively warring against and dismantling the powers of darkness over the nation.

He, as *one man*, challenged and defeated 450 false prophets of Baal upon Mt. Carmel. (We will look deeper into this "*one man*" in a later section). This is the one single event that changed the nation and turned Israel back to God, and also revealed the power and glory of God to the people.

Some of the legitimate questions that can be asked concerning this awesome prophet of God could be – what

---

[12] 1 Kings 17 & 18

was the operating systems of this man's life? What made him function the way that he did? Was he endowed with some kind of special anointing that we can never posses? And the list can go on; however, we want to look a bit deeper into the life of this major Prophet of God and see the foundation of his life.

He was a man of purity; living a sanctified life

This is reflected; by the very first thing that he did which was to call the people to make a choice between Baal and God:

"Then it happened, when Ahab saw Elijah, that Ahab said to him, "Is that you, O troubler of Israel?" And he answered, *"I have not troubled Israel, but you and your father's house have, in that you have forsaken the commandments of the LORD* and you have followed the Baals. Now therefore, send and gather all Israel to me on Mount Carmel, the four hundred and fifty Prophets of Baal, and the four hundred Prophets of Asherah, who eat at Jezebel's table." So Ahab sent for all the children of Israel, and gathered the Prophets together on Mount Carmel. *And Elijah came to all the people, and said, "How long will you falter between two opinions? If the LORD is God, follow Him*; but if Baal, follow him." But the people answered him not a word." 1 Kings 18:17-21 (Italics added)

The spirit and power of Elijah goes against complacency and worldliness. It confronts the religious spirit that makes people hearers of the word and not doers.

It attacks the very demonic power that causes the "word of God to be ineffective":

"Then the Pharisees and scribes asked Him, "Why do Your disciples not walk according to the tradition of the elders, but eat bread with unwashed hands?" He answered and said to them. "Well did Isaiah prophesy of you hypocrites, as it is written: 'This people *honors Me with their lips, But their heart is far from Me.* And in vain they worship Me, *Teaching as doctrines the commandments of men.'* "For laying aside the commandment of God, you hold the tradition of men-- the washing of pitchers and cups, and many other such things you do." And He said to them, "All too well *you reject the commandment of God, that you may keep your tradition.* For Moses said, 'Honor your father and your mother'; and, 'He who curses father or mother, let him be put to death.' But you say, 'If a man says to his father or mother, "Whatever profit you might have received from me is Corban"--' (that is, a gift to God), then you no longer let him do anything for his father or his mother, *making the word of God of no effect through your tradition which you have handed down.* And many such things you do." Mark 7:5-13 (Italics added)

It also attacks that spirit that causes one to have a *"form of godliness, but denying the power thereof"* - 2 Timothy 3:5. It draws a line between the holy and the profane and pushes people to a place of sanctification, purity and unswerving commitment to the Lord.

This was also reflected in him restoring the Altars of the Lord – the true, pure places of worship:

"And he *repaired the altar of the LORD* that was broken down.   And Elijah took twelve stones, according to the number of the tribes of the sons of Jacob, to whom the word of the LORD had come, saying, "Israel shall be your name." *Then with the stones he built an altar in the name of the LORD..."*
1 Kings 18:30-32 (Italics added)

Altars represent places of sacrifice, purity, sanctification and true commitment!   The Elijah spirit always seeks to push people to a return to the Altar:

"In those days John the Baptist came preaching in the wilderness of Judea, and saying, "Repent, for the kingdom of heaven is at hand!" For this is he who was spoken of by the Prophet Isaiah, saying: "The voice of one crying in the wilderness: *'Prepare the way of the LORD; Make His paths straight."*   Matthew 3:1-3 (Italics added)

"I beseech you therefore, brethren, by the mercies of God, that *you present your bodies a living sacrifice, holy, acceptable to God,* which is your reasonable service. And *do not be conformed to this world, but be transformed by the renewing of your mind,* that you may prove what is that good and acceptable and perfect will of God." Romans 12:1-2 (Italics added)

Elijah restores the Altar and then goes on to prepare the

sacrifice. Through the apostolic restoration that is taking place we are beginning to see pure worship restored, pure communion restored, pure commitment restored to the people of God. There is a new breed of Christians arising in the earth that will not compromise and will walk in purity!

He was a true Leader

"Now therefore, send and gather all Israel to me on Mount Carmel, the four hundred and fifty Prophets of Baal, and the four hundred Prophets of Asherah, who eat at Jezebel's table... Then *Elijah said to all the people, "Come near to me."* So all the people came near to him." 1 Kings 18:19, 30 (Italics added)

This is the heart of a true leader. He does not send people away in their confusion and sin, but seeks to draw them near. Elijah did not consider himself to be the only righteous man in Israel, or the man of God for the hour or thought everyone else was not walking accurately in the things of God so may the judgment of God fall upon them, they deserved it. No, instead he lays his life on the line for the people of God, and presents true leadership to them; he identifies with the people and restores the true government of God in their lives.

The true Elijah/prophetic anointing while it is aggressive and confrontational operates from a heart that loves people. It wants to confront people with the view of bringing them closer to God. Apostles Peter and John bring out this dimension very clearly in their account in *Acts 3:1-10*, which we will look at in greater, detail later on.

- **He was a man that knew how to draw near to God**
  "And it came to pass, at the time of the offering of the evening sacrifice, *that Elijah the Prophet came near* and said, "LORD God of Abraham, Isaac, and Israel, let it be known this day that You are God in Israel and I am Your servant, and that I have done all these things at Your word. Hear me, O LORD, hear me, that this people may know that You are the LORD God, and that You have turned their hearts back to You again." Then the fire of the LORD fell and consumed the burnt sacrifice, and the wood and the stones and the dust, and it licked up the water that was in the trench. Now when all the people saw it, they fell on their faces; and they said, "The LORD, He is God! The LORD, He is God!"" 1 Kings 18:36-39 (Italics added)

Verse 36 gives us the key to unlock the door to the Power of God! At the time of the evening sacrifice Elijah *draws near to God!*

This is awesome, for as we draw near to God we cannot help but be pure and holy and this releases the Lord to do great and mighty things through us. For the word of God says that as we "draw near to God, He will draw near to us"[13] and when this happens cleansing and purification take place, resulting in the Lord elevating us:

※ *"Draw near to God* and He will draw near to you. *Cleanse your hands,* you sinners; and *purify your hearts*, you double-minded. Lament and mourn and

---

[13] James 4:8-10

weep! Let your laughter be turned to mourning and your joy to gloom. *Humble yourselves in the sight of the Lord*, and He will lift you up." James 4:8-10 (Italics added)

We are not called to pray empty prayers that cannot breakthrough! We are called to pray with strength, wisdom and intensity.

Elijah's Prayer
He addresses a patriarchal God! "Lord God of Abraham, Isaac and Israel..." 1 Kings 18:36 He knows that God is a God who has worked throughout the generations and can work in his generation as well.

He goes on - *let it be known this day!* Not in somebody else's day! *Today in our day!*

Oh! I tell you, this is part of the *"apostolic grace"*, it has the ability to bring things into *today* – it loves to bring clarity! It loves to say, "This is that which was spoken."[14]

Remember the word of God declares to us that Elijah was a man with a nature like ours – James 5:17-18:

"Elijah was a man with *a nature like ours,* and he prayed earnestly that it would not rain; and it did not rain on the land for three years and six months. And he prayed again, and the heaven gave rain, and the earth produced its fruit." (Italics added)

---

[14] Acts 2:16

Yes, it is true he was a human being just like us, he flowed and functioned in a crazy mixed up world just like ours, he had to confront and deal with the issues of his day, - just like us, he had his areas of shortcomings just like us, *but* God worked through his life and He can work through ours, as we surrender our all on the Altar for Him.

Pitfalls Of The Elijah Spirit

It is vital that we look at some of the pitfalls we need to avoid, with this end-time anointing. Elijah moved from the mountaintop of victory to the abyss of defeat and death[15], and we need to uncover the reason, so as to avoid making the same errors. As the word of God declares to us that:

> *"All Scripture is given by inspiration of God,* and is profitable for doctrine, for reproof, for correction, for instruction in righteousness, that the man of God may be complete, thoroughly equipped for every good work."* 2 Timothy 3:16-17 (Italics added)

One Man!   *danger !*

Herein lies one of the greatest traps of the Elijah spirit that we need to avoid in this apostolic and prophetic restoration.   Elijah became so engulfed in his own significance and walk that he thought he was the *only man alive that was walking accurately in the will of God!*

> "And there he went into a cave, and spent the night in that place; and behold, the word of the LORD came to him, and He said to him, "What are you doing here,

---

[15] 1 Kings 19:4

Elijah?" So he said, "I have been very zealous for the LORD God of hosts; for the children of Israel have forsaken Your covenant, torn down Your altars, and killed Your Prophets with the sword. *I alone am left*; and they seek to take my life."   1 Kings 19:9-10 (Italics added)

God's Response!
"Yet *I have reserved seven thousand* in Israel, all whose knees have not bowed to Baal, and every mouth that has not kissed him." 1 Kings 19:18 (Italics added)

In essence what God was saying to him was "listen Elijah, do not even think that it was your "*one man*" heroics that accomplished these mighty acts. I want you to understand that there was a "*many-membered man*" that accomplished this mighty and awesome exploit for Me. Elijah you were only the "spearhead" but I had a shaft of "seven thousand" attached to you assisting in accomplishing the task. As a matter of fact Elijah's tenure on earth did not last much past the unhealthy mindset of him being the only one that was standing for God. The Lord appears to him in 1 Kings 19 and declares the end of his tenure:

"Then the LORD said to him: "Go, return on your way to the Wilderness of Damascus; and when you arrive, anoint Hazael as king over Syria. Also you shall anoint Jehu the son of Nimshi as king over Israel. *And Elisha* the son of Shaphat of Abel Meholah *you shall anoint as prophet in your place*." 1 Kings 19:15-16 (Italics added)

The outcome of the directive saw Elijah being taken and Elisha stepping into his function, which also will be dealt with in more detail later on.

It is like so many churches and ministries today who believe that they are the only ones doing the will of God. Some ministries hold "centre stage" and they assume that they are the only right ones.

Let me share with you an imagery the Lord gave me recently. He showed me a city and in that city there were several containers of varying sizes all filed with seawater. Then He showed me the ocean and said to me that it represented His Kingdom, and then proceeded to explain an interesting scenario. He said if you were to test the water in each of the containers, it would produce the exact same results as that of the ocean. He said therein lies the problem with most churches. They assume that, because they consist of the same composition as that of the Kingdom, they are the "church or ministry" in that nation. They call themselves "*the territorial church*" of that region or nation, the Lord continued saying to me, which is the same as assuming that any one of the containers that was filled with seawater was the ocean. The point is, no matter how much you think you, as an individual are serving God, He always has a "*seven thousand*" walking in His will and creating the necessary openings and breakthroughs for "*Elijah*" to be successful in establishing God's ordained will. I hope you get the point! It is time for churches and ministries in every nation to really wise up and get the message – we are all in this together, and it is time to place all on the Altar and walk in purity, righteousness, holiness, in the bond of peace and in unison get the job done. I know it is easier said than done, but

God by His Holy Spirit is releasing an anointing in this hour for it to be accomplished.

After doing great exploits for God the enemy did just what he does to every one of us after a resounding victory over his domain. He tries to negate the impact, by causing us to turn our attention away from the Lord and His voice, to our importance and significance in the working of God. This is what happened as soon as Elijah destroyed the 450 false prophets of Baal, and caused an awesome victory to come to the people of God and returned them to the realm of *purity*. The devil stirred up Jezebel and she declared:

"Then Jezebel sent a messenger to Elijah, saying, "So let the gods do to me, and more also, if I do not make your life as the life of one of them by tomorrow about this time." 1 Kings 19:2

As we read on in the chapter we see that Elijah fled in an attempt to save his life and fell from a mountaintop of victory to the abyss of defeat and death – He just came down from Mt. Carmel where he birthed in prayer, another mighty move of God, to a place where he was fleeing for his life and wishing he could die, and entered into a false sense of self pity:

"And when he saw that, he arose and ran for his life, and went to Beersheba, which belongs to Judah, and left his servant there. But he himself went a day's journey into the wilderness, and came and sat down under a broom tree. *And he prayed that he might die,* and said, "It is enough! *Now, LORD, take my life,*

for I am no better than my fathers!"   1 Kings 19:3-4
(Italics added)

Understanding The Spirit Of Jezebel

The name Jezebel means – "un-co-habited", even
though she was married. So in essence Jezebel means "one
who is uncovered or one that will not submit to authority".
Please understand that this is not a woman thing, it is a
spirit that affects both male and female. It is an unclean
spirit that seeks to manipulate and control governmental
authority, and can only function effectively whenever there
is weak leadership such as the nature of Ahab's:

> "But there was no one like Ahab who sold himself to
> do wickedness in the sight of the LORD, *because
> Jezebel his wife stirred him up.* And he behaved very
> abominably in following idols, according to all that the
> Amorites had done, whom the LORD had cast out
> before the children of Israel." 1 Kings 21:25-26 (Italics
> added)

She entered the life of Israel through the gateway of
marriage:

> "In the thirty-eighth year of Asa king of Judah, *Ahab
> the son of Omri became king over Israel*; and Ahab the
> son of Omri reigned over Israel in Samaria twenty-two
> years. Now Ahab the son of Omri did evil in the sight
> of the LORD, more than all who were before him. And
> it came to pass, as though it had been a trivial thing for
> him to walk in the sins of Jeroboam the son of Nebat,
> that *he took as wife Jezebel* the daughter of Ethbaal,

king of the Sidonians; and he went and served Baal and worshiped him." 1 Kings 16:29-31 (Italics added)

Ahab married Jezebel in total contradiction to the law laid down by God, which states:

"When the LORD your God brings you into the land which you go to possess, and has cast out many nations before you, the Hittites and the Girgashites and the Amorites and the Canaanites and the Perizzites and the Hivites and the Jebusites, seven nations greater and mightier than you, and when the LORD your God delivers them over to you, you shall conquer them and utterly destroy them. You shall make no covenant with them nor show mercy to them. *Nor shall you make marriages with them.* You shall not give your daughter to their son, nor take their daughter for your son. For they will turn your sons away from following Me, to serve other gods; so the anger of the LORD will be aroused against you and destroy you suddenly." Deuteronomy 7:1-4 (Italics added)

She established a false system of government, by having [16]four hundred and fifty prophets personally serve her in her evil ways.   [17]Jezebel attacked and massacred the legitimate, God-ordained authority of her day - it is a type of spirit that still attacks true, legitimate, God-ordained, ministry. Ministry that has vision and that can discern the heart and mind of God. She represents a bold, demonic authority that wants to

---

[16] 1 Kings 18:19
[17] 1 Kings 18:4

kill, legitimate God-ordained ministry and does not want any form of retaliation.

In the following passage of scripture the true nature and foundation of the spirit of Jezebel is exposed:

to do with BIRTH RITE

"And it came to pass after these things that Naboth the Jezreelite had a vineyard which was in Jezreel, next to the palace of Ahab king of Samaria. So Ahab spoke to Naboth, saying, "Give me your vineyard, that I may have it for a vegetable garden, because it is near, next to my house; and for it I will give you a vineyard better than it. Or, if it seems good to you, I will give you its worth in money." *But Naboth said to Ahab, "The LORD forbid that I should give the inheritance of my fathers to you!"* So Ahab went into his house sullen and displeased because of the word which Naboth the Jezreelite had spoken to him; for he had said, "I will not give you the inheritance of my fathers." And he lay down on his bed, and turned away his face, and would eat no food. But Jezebel his wife came to him, and said to him, "Why is your spirit so sullen that you eat no food?" He said to her, "Because I spoke to Naboth the Jezreelite, and said to him, 'Give me your vineyard for money; or else, if it pleases you, I will give you another vineyard for it.' And he answered, 'I will not give you my vineyard.' *"Then Jezebel his wife said to him, "You now exercise authority over Israel*! Arise, eat food, and let your heart be cheerful; *I will give you the vineyard* of Naboth the Jezreelite." *And she wrote letters in Ahab's name, sealed them with his seal*, and sent the letters to the elders and the nobles who were dwelling in the city with Naboth. She wrote in the letters, saying, Proclaim a fast, and seat Naboth with high honor among the people; and seat two men, scoundrels, before him to bear witness against him, saying, "You have blasphemed God and the king." Then take him out, and stone him, that he may die. So the men of his city, the elders and nobles who were inhabitants of his city, did as Jezebel had sent to them, as it was written in the letters which she had sent to them. They proclaimed a fast, and seated Naboth with high honor among the people. And two men, scoundrels, came in and sat before him; and the scoundrels witnessed against him, against Naboth, in the presence of the people, saying, "Naboth has blasphemed God and the king!" Then they took him outside the city and stoned him with stones, so that he died. Then they sent to Jezebel, saying, "Naboth has been stoned and is dead." And it came to pass, *when Jezebel heard that Naboth had been stoned and was dead, that Jezebel said to Ahab, "Arise, take possession of the vineyard of Naboth the Jezreelite, which he refused to give you for money; for Naboth is not alive, but dead."* So it was, when Ahab heard that Naboth was dead, that Ahab got up and went down to take possession of the vineyard of Naboth the Jezreelite." 1 Kings 21:1-16 (Italics added)

Points to extract:
- She married into weak leadership
- She sought to manipulate and control leadership
- She usurped authority to conduct evil

She was seemingly a loving wife who was willing to get

her husband anything he wanted – a false display of loyalty.

The Lord warned us of this spirit entering into the end-time church:

self promotion?

"Nevertheless I have a few things against you, because you allow *that woman Jezebel, who calls herself a Prophetess, to teach and seduce* My servants to commit sexual immorality and eat things sacrificed to idols." Revelation 2:20 (Italics added) *– agree with digest – take in*

It disguises itself in the prophetic realm – She calls herself a prophetess in direct opposition to the true Elijah anointing and spirit of the last days.

It rises up in an attempt to bring revelation to the Church by means of teaching – representing a [18]counterfeit of the true apostolic ministry being restored in the last days.

She uses seduction as her main tactic. Seduction is a cunning, well-planned, system of attack with the sole intent of misleading and deceiving.

---

[18] 2 Corinthians 11:13-15

Chapter 2
Defeating The Spirit of Jezebel

It will take a double portion of the prophetic anointing, and the kingly dimension of the apostolic anointing to defeat and destroy the spirit of Jezebel. Even as it was in Elijah's day, so it is in our day. Let us revisit those events so that we can be instructed in the divine technology with which to defeat the spirit of Jezebel.

1 Kings 19:11-18 records the account of Elijah's life after killing the false prophets of Baal and fleeing from Jezebel and wanting to die:

"Then He said, "Go out, and stand on the mountain before the LORD." And behold, the LORD passed by, and a great and strong wind tore into the mountains and broke the rocks in pieces before the LORD, but the LORD was not in the wind; and after the wind an earthquake, but the LORD was not in the earthquake; and after the earthquake a fire, but the LORD was not in the fire; and after the fire a still small voice. So it was, when Elijah heard it, that he wrapped his face in his mantle and went out and stood in the entrance of the cave. Suddenly a voice came to him, and said, "What are you doing here, Elijah?" And he said, "I have been very zealous for the LORD God of hosts; because the children of Israel have forsaken Your covenant, torn down Your altars, and killed Your Prophets with the sword. I alone am left; and they seek to take my life." *Then the LORD said to him:* "Go, return on your way to the Wilderness of Damascus; and when you arrive, *anoint Hazael as king over Syria.* Also you shall *anoint Jehu* the son of Nimshi *as king over Israel. And Elisha* the son of Shaphat of Abel Meholah *you shall anoint as Prophet in your place.* It shall be that whoever escapes the sword of Hazael, Jehu will kill; and whoever escapes from the sword of Jehu, Elisha will kill." 1 Kings 19:11-17 (Italics added)

God mandated Elijah to:
- Anoint Hazael as king over Syria
- Anoint Jehu as king over Israel
- Anoint Elisha the son of Shaphat of Abel Meholah to be Prophet in his place.

✳ Elijah only fulfills the third command of his prophetic mandate[19].

A very interesting point of note

---

[19] 2 Kings 2: 9-15

Elisha means, "God is (his or for) Salvation and Abel Meholah means "Meadow of Dancing". - The call and anointing comes to Elisha while he is thoroughly engaged in tending his father's oxen (doing the work of the Father – hands on the plough) with great joy. That's how the call of God comes, while we are busying ourselves doing the work of the ministry. It does not come from observation or seeking recognition and position. Elijah is taken up in a chariot of fire and Elisha steps into a *double portion* of his anointing (This is a double portion of the prophetic anointing). He then goes on to fulfill Elijah's mandate by anointing Hazael king over Syria and also anoints Jehu as king.

Let Us Focus On Jehu's Anointing

"And Elisha the Prophet called one of the sons of the Prophets, and said to him, "Get yourself ready, take this flask of oil in your hand, and go to Ramoth Gilead. Now when you arrive at that place, look there for Jehu the son of Jehoshaphat, the son of Nimshi, and go in and make him rise up from among his associates, and take him to an *inner room*. Then take the flask of oil, and pour it on his head, and say, 'Thus says the LORD: "I have anointed you king over Israel." ' Then open the door and flee, and do not delay." So the young man, the servant of the Prophet, went to Ramoth Gilead. And when he arrived, there were the captains of the army sitting; and he said, "I have a message for you, Commander." Jehu said, "For which one of us?" And he said, "For you, Commander." Then he arose and went into the house. And he poured the oil on his head, and said to him, "Thus says the LORD God of Israel: 'I have anointed you king over the people of the LORD, over Israel. *You shall strike down the house of Ahab your master,* that I may avenge the blood of My servants the Prophets, and the blood of all the servants of the LORD, at the hand of Jezebel. For the whole house of Ahab shall perish; and I will cut off from Ahab all the males in Israel, both bond and free. So I will make the house of Ahab like the house of Jeroboam the son of Nebat, and like the house of Baasha the son of Ahijah. *The dogs shall eat Jezebel* on the plot of ground at Jezreel, and there shall be none to bury her.' " And he opened the door and fled." 2 Kings 9:1-10 (Italics added)

Points of Note:

- Elisha himself does not anoint Jehu – he sends one of the sons of the prophets – verse 1! This speaks about the power of relationship within the framework of training, accountability, submission, etc. There are some things we will never be able to do for God apart from this!

- Jehu was separated from his fellowmen and taken into an *"Inner Room"* – verse 2! This *"Inner Room Anointing"* is very vital in the call of God. This is where we receive the power to do works of service. It is here we receive our mandate, revelation and the technology for success. Remember what Jesus instructed us in Matthew 10:27 *"Whatever I tell you in the dark, speak in the light; and what you hear in the ear, preach on the housetops.*

- Jehu then receives his general mandate: 2 Kings 9:6 "I

have anointed you king over the people of the Lord, over Israel" – this is very general! It is similar to being anointed and being told "for I anointed you to be a man/woman of God, and I have released to you gifts and abilities to accomplish all that I would have thee to, etc, etc…" – very general!

- Jehu then receives his *specific mandate*: 2 Kings 9:6 *"You shall strike down the house of Ahab your master, that I may avenge the blood of My servants the Prophets, and the blood of all the servants of the LORD, at the hand of Jezebel."* This specific mandate has its root in a previous sequence of events, which is most times the case. *God did this because of the following*:

"And it came to pass after these things that Naboth the Jezreelite had a vineyard which was in Jezreel, next to the palace of Ahab king of Samaria. So Ahab spoke to Naboth, saying, "Give me your vineyard, that I may have it for a vegetable garden, because it is near, next to my house; and for it I will give you a vineyard better than it. Or, if it seems good to you, I will give you its worth in money." But Naboth said to Ahab, "The LORD forbid that I should give the inheritance of my fathers to you!" So Ahab went into his house sullen and displeased because of the word which Naboth the Jezreelite had spoken to him; for he had said, "I will not give you the inheritance of my fathers." And he lay down on his bed, and turned away his face, and would eat no food. But Jezebel his wife came to him, and said to him, "Why is your spirit so sullen that you eat no food?" He said to her, "Because I spoke to Naboth the Jezreelite, and said to him, 'Give me your vineyard for money; or else, if it pleases you, I will give you another vineyard for it.' And he answered, 'I will not give you my vineyard.' "Then Jezebel his wife said to him, "You now exercise authority over Israel! Arise, eat food, and let your heart be cheerful; I will give you the vineyard of Naboth the Jezreelite."   And she wrote letters in Ahab's name, sealed them with his seal, and sent the letters to the elders and the nobles who were dwelling in the city with Naboth. She wrote in the letters, saying, Proclaim a fast, and seat Naboth with high honor among the people; and seat two men, scoundrels, before him to bear witness against him, saying, "You have blasphemed God and the king." Then take him out, and stone him, that he may die. So the men of his city, the elders and nobles who were inhabitants of his city, did as Jezebel had sent to them, as it was written in the letters which she had sent to them. They proclaimed a fast, and seated Naboth with high honor among the people.   And two men, scoundrels, came in and sat before him; and the scoundrels witnessed against him, against Naboth, in the presence of the people, saying, "Naboth blasphemed God and the king!" Then they took him outside the city and stoned him with stones, so that he died. Then they sent to Jezebel, saying, "Naboth has been stoned and is dead."   And it came to pass, when Jezebel heard that Naboth had been stoned and was dead, that Jezebel said to Ahab, "Arise, take possession of the vineyard of Naboth the Jezreelite, which he refused to give you for money; for Naboth is not alive, but dead." So it was, when Ahab heard that Naboth was dead, that Ahab got up and went down to take possession of the vineyard of Naboth the Jezreelite. Then the word of the LORD came to Elijah the Tishbite, saying, "Arise, go down to meet Ahab king of Israel, who lives in Samaria. There he is, in the vineyard of Naboth, where he has gone down to take possession of it. You shall speak to him, saying, 'Thus says the LORD: "Have you murdered and also taken possession?" ' And you shall speak to him, saying, 'Thus says the LORD: "In the place where dogs licked the blood of Naboth, dogs shall lick your blood, even yours." ""Then Ahab said to Elijah, "Have you found me, O my enemy?" And he answered, "I have found you, because you have sold yourself to do evil in the sight of the LORD: 'Behold, I will bring calamity on you. I will take away your posterity, and will cut off from Ahab every male in Israel, both bond and free. I will make your house like the house of Jeroboam the son of Nebat, and like the house of Baasha the son of Ahijah, because of the provocation with which you have provoked Me to anger, and made Israel sin.' "And concerning Jezebel the LORD also spoke, saying, 'The dogs shall eat Jezebel by the wall of Jezreel.' "The dogs shall eat whoever belongs to Ahab and dies in the city, and the birds of the air shall eat whoever dies in the field." 1 Kings 21: 1-24

It will augur well for us to take a closer look at how Jehu accomplished the God given mandate that was placed upon him. We want to approach this from the understanding that the [20]*godly kings* in the Old Testament were a type of the apostles in the New Testament and can give us valuable operational technology for apostles today.

The background to Jehu's reign was – there existed in Israel at that time the impure and incapable leadership in the Jezebel/Ahab's administration.   The Word of God declares:

> "*Woe to you, O land, when your king is a child*, And your princes feast in the morning! Blessed are you, O land, when your king is the son of nobles, And your princes feast at the proper time--For strength and not for drunkenness!" Ecclesiastes 10:16-17 (Italics added)

Jezebel (*a false governmental voice*) was in power and thereby released all kinds of demonic powers over the land. Demonic powers were in the gates of the city and the Lord had established a covenant with Abraham that the people of God would always possess the gates of their enemies:

> "Then the Angel of the LORD called to Abraham a second time out of heaven, and said: "By Myself I have sworn, says the LORD, because you have done this thing, and have not withheld your son, your only son-- blessing I will bless you, and in multiplying I will multiply your descendants as the stars of the heaven and as the sand which is on the seashore; *and your descendants shall possess the gate of their enemies.*"

[20] For more teaching on this subject you can read Dr. Roger Sapp's book "The Last Apostles on Earth" – ISBN 1-56043-568-2

Genesis 22:15-17 (Italics added)

"And they blessed Rebekah and said to her: "Our sister, may you become The mother of thousands of ten thousands; And may *your descendants possess the gates of those who hate them*." Genesis 24:60 (Italics added)

In establishing Jehu as [21]king (a type of the apostolic) the Lord would ensure that the enemy was defeated and true governance returned to Israel.

In like manner we are being raised up by God to take away the authority from demonic elders and establish the government of God in the earth! Jehu was anointed in the *"inner room"* where he was equipped for service!

speaks of intimate relationship with God - intimacy - Knows God

He then steps out and fulfills Elijah's mandate to the letter. In order to accomplish this he had to make sure that he was intensely focused! He was about to confront one of the strongest demonic powers of the day.

In order to fulfill any God given mandate one must be intensely *focused*.

Focus - a concentration of intent upon specific mandates or purposes. It is similar to a *magnifying glass being used on paper in the sun.*

Focus is the key to success and this is true for any area

---

[21] For more teaching on this subject you can read Dr. Roger Sapp's book "The Last Apostles on Earth" – ISBN 1-56043-568-2

of one's life. *Loss of Focus* causes one's strength to depart and defeat to step in. ✳ This is one of the enemy's main tactics, causing us to loose Focus[22].

As we read through the account of Jehu's fulfillment of the prophetic word given to him, we will realize how focused he was in accomplishing the task at hand[23].

Conversely if we study the life of Saul we can see the results of the [24]loss of focus in fulfilling a God-given mandate.

The Need Of The Apostolic And Prophetic To Destroy The Jezebel Spirit

As we carefully look back at the chain of events that took place to dislodge and destroy Jezebel in the Old Testament, we would understand the significance of the *apostolic* and *prophetic* in destroying the spirit of Jezebel in the last-day church, in order to ensure that purity exists within her ranks.

Long before Jehu was anointed to be king over Israel ✳ God had already declared the demise and total destruction of the Jezebel/Ahab administration:

"Then the word of the LORD came to Elijah the Tishbite, saying, "Arise, go down to meet Ahab king of Israel, who lives in Samaria. There he is, in the vine-

---

[22] Hebrews 10:35-39
[23] II Kings 9
[24] I Samuel 15

yard of Naboth, where he has gone down to take possession of it. You shall speak to him, saying, 'Thus says the LORD: "Have you murdered and also taken possession?" ' And you shall speak to him, saying, 'Thus says the LORD: "In the place where dogs licked the blood of Naboth, dogs shall lick your blood, even yours." '"Then Ahab said to Elijah, "Have you found me, O my enemy?" And he answered, "I have found you, because you have sold yourself to do evil in the sight of the LORD: 'Behold, I will bring calamity on you I will take away your posterity, and will cut off from Ahab every male in Israel, both bond and free. I will make your house like the house of Jeroboam the son of Nebat, and like the house of Baasha the son of Ahijah, because of the provocation with which you have provoked Me to anger, and made Israel sin.' "And concerning Jezebel the LORD also spoke, saying, 'The dogs shall eat Jezebel by the wall of Jezreel.' "The dogs shall eat whoever belongs to Ahab and dies in the city, and the birds of the air shall eat whoever dies in the field." 1 Kings 21:17-24

✳ **In fulfilling the prophetic word** spoken by Elijah to the Jezebel/Ahab administration, God had to use Elisha, who received a double portion of Elijah's prophetic anointing, and Jehu, who received an apostolic (kingly) anointing in the *"inner room"*. Elisha prophesied it, and Jehu accomplished it. As was said before, the prophetic has the anointing to foresee and declare, while the apostolic has the anointing to bring to pass what the prophetic saw. Hence the reason, the prophetic and apostolic must function as a team.

God, by His Spirit, in these last days has released the prophetic and apostolic anointing to destroy the spirit of Jezebel – a false prophetic/apostolic spirit – in His Church. He declared that:

"And to the angel of the church in Thyatira write, 'These things says the Son of God, who has eyes like a flame of fire, and His feet like fine brass: "I know your works, love, service, faith, and your patience; and as for your works, the last are more than the first. Nevertheless I have a few things against you, because *you allow that woman Jezebel, who calls herself a Prophetess, [false prophetic ministry] to teach [a type of false apostolic ministry]* and *seduce My servants* to commit sexual immorality and eat things sacrificed to idols. And I gave her time to repent of her sexual immorality, and she did not repent. Indeed I will cast her into a sickbed, and those who commit adultery with her into great tribulation, unless they repent of their deeds. *I will kill her children with death*, and all the churches shall know that I am He who searches the minds and hearts. And I will give to each one of you according to your works." Revelation 2:18-23 (Italics and Parenthesis added)

Points to note:
- The spirit of Jezebel will be active in the Last-Day Church.
- That spirit will manifest itself in the prophetic and apostolic realm.
- It will carry a strong seductive emphasis.
- It will be empowered to attempt to cause the servants

of God to commit sexual (also spiritual) immorality.
- It will also have a strong spirit of deception.

This is why there will be such a strong emphasis, to try them who say they are apostles. Please understand that not everyone who carries the title "*apostle*" is sent by God:

> "To the angel of the church of Ephesus write, 'These things says He who holds the seven stars in His right hand, who walks in the midst of the seven golden lampstands: "I know your works, your labor, your patience, and that you cannot bear those who are evil. And *you have tested those who say they are Apostles and are not, and have found them liars.*" Revelation 2:1-2 (Italics added)

The Apostle Paul warned us of these false apostles and false ministers rising up in the church:

> "For I consider that I am not at all inferior to the most eminent Apostles. Even though I am untrained in speech, yet I am not in knowledge. But we have been thoroughly manifested among you in all things. Did I commit sin in humbling myself that you might be exalted, because I preached the gospel of God to you free of charge? "...But what I do, I will also continue to do, that I may cut off the opportunity from those who desire an opportunity to be regarded just as we are in the things of which they boast. *For such are false Apostles, deceitful workers, transforming themselves into Apostles of Christ.* And no wonder! For Satan himself transforms himself into an angel of light.

Therefore it is no great thing if his ministers also transform themselves into ministers of righteousness, whose end will be according to their works." 2 Corinthians 11:5-7, 12-15 (Italics added)

Again let me re-emphasize - it will take "**Apostolic Purity**", wisdom and warfare strength, along with prophetic vision and tenacity, to defeat and destroy the spirit of Jezebel in these last days.

Remember the wise words of the Apostle Paul:

"For the weapons of our warfare are not carnal but mighty in God for pulling down strongholds, casting down arguments and every high thing that exalts itself against the knowledge of God, bringing every thought into captivity to the obedience of Christ, and being ready to punish all disobedience when your obedience is fulfilled." 2 Corinthians 10:4-6

A note of caution in trying them who say they are apostles – while not everyone who carries the title is an apostle; we need to understand that this does not make them a false minister or a false Christian. Some people will be misguided or misdirected, and we need to discern accurately in order to rightly restore the person. As with every move of God, there is emphasis placed on what the Holy Spirit is seeking to accomplish. In this case it is the restoration of apostles, which has become a *"buzz word"* in the church, and because of this, many are being called apostle – some rightly so while others are being called this erroneously. This is why we will need wisdom and the true [25]*"fathering anointing"* to discern and implement the right course of action in dealing with them who say they are apostles and are not.

*we need WISDOM
true fathering anointing*

---

[25] You can read the author's book "Five Pillars of The Apostolic" for a more in-depth analysis on the "fathering anointing".

Chapter 3
Working A Work In Our Time!

God, by His Holy Spirit, is indeed working a work in our day. This is the most glorious day the Church has ever seen. The Church of Jesus Christ is maturing and is preparing the way for the return of our King! The spirit of Elijah is upon us, as we function as John the Baptist! *vision Regina SK Jan 11.2006 standing on a threshold - much activity inside (heaven) God preparing for the*

I believe that we are at the threshold of [26]"New Things" in God. As I sought the Lord, the Holy Spirit impressed upon my spirit these two scriptures: *sons of God to be manifest-*

"Look among the nations and watch—Be utterly astounded! For *I will work a work in your days* Which you would not believe, though it were told you." Habakkuk 1:5 (Italics added)

=69=

---

[26] Isaiah 48:6-7

There is such a stirring of the Spirit of God, it is difficult to adequately articulate. It will seem as though there is a *"divine buzz"* in the spirit realm, as the Lord continues to prepare a people that will literally shock this planet.

I believe the words that were spoken by the Prophet Habakkuk are applicable to us today. There is still a **"now"** application to it.   However, there must be a constant agreement with the Lord for its fulfillment and we must not enter into the realm of unbelief.

Unbelief

This has always been one of the greatest stumbling blocks to any move of God. You will find that it was a pivotal factor in the demise of the children of Israel on their way to the Promised Land[27] They were destroyed in the wilderness because of it:

> "So we see that they could not enter because of unbelief." Hebrews 3:19

Jesus had to confront and deal with that same spirit in His day:

> "And when He had come to His own country, He taught them in their synagogue, so that they were astonished and said, "Where did this Man get this wisdom and these mighty works? Is this not the carpenter's son? Is not His mother called Mary? And

---

[27] Hebrews 3:1-19

His brothers James, Joses, Simon, and Judas? And His sisters, are they not all with us? Where then did this Man get all these things?" So they were offended at Him. But Jesus said to them, "A Prophet is not without honor except in his own country and in his own house." Now *He did not do many mighty works there because of their unbelief."* Matthew 13:54-58 (Italics added)

"Now He could do no mighty work there, except that He laid His hands on a few sick people and healed them. *And He marvelled because of their unbelief."* Mark 6:5-6 (Italics added)   *wickedness of unbelief!*

Today God is speaking – through the mouths of His servants, do not harden your heart but hear what the Spirit of God is saying to His Church. Remember we are shaped by what we believe. You are what you eat!

In Mark's gospel we clearly see that the creative, miracle-working power of God is activated by our *"belief system"*:

"Later He appeared to the eleven as they sat at the table; and He rebuked their unbelief and hardness of heart, because they did not believe those who had seen Him after He had risen. And He said to them, "Go into all the world and preach the gospel to every creature. He who believes and is baptized will be saved; but he who does not believe will be condemned. And *these signs will follow those who believe*: In My name they will cast out demons; they will speak with new tongues; they will take up serpents; and if they drink anything deadly, it will by no means hurt them; they will lay hands on the sick, and they will recover." Mark 16:14-18 (Italics added)

We need to fully understand that the Lord will not move in a territory, region or people, unless He finds someone to partner with Him[28]. The Lord is always looking over the planet to find a people that will believe Him for His glory to manifest in that place. *The very structures in which we live*, seek to limit us in depending and believing in our natural ability instead of in God.

If we are not careful, we can allow ourselves to struggle with believing in God. The very thought of God using us to establish His glory and movements in the earth, could sometimes seem remote and very alien, and we are oft times encouraged to pray with a "hit and miss" approach. "Well if God wants it to happen it will happen; if not, well it is up to Him" we hear some around us declaring.

I tell you, that the move of God will only come as we partner with Him and begin to *"boldly command it"*.

The Lord declared to us through His word that He requires us to be *bold* in seeking Him[29]. This brings us to the second scriptural reference:

"Thus says the LORD, The Holy One of Israel, and his Maker: *"Ask Me of things to come concerning My sons; And concerning the work of My hands, you*

---

[28] Amos 3:3,7
[29] Hebrews 4:11-16

command Me. I have made the earth, And created man on it. I—My hands-- stretched out the heavens, And all their host I have commanded." Isaiah 45:11-12 (Italics added)

This chapter begins with a powerful proclamation by God, Himself declaring that Cyrus was His Anointed. We can most certainly apply this scripture to the Church of Jesus Christ in the earth, of which we are a part. The Church is God's Anointed in this hour. These are apostolic days in which the Spirit of God has released His grace for us to seek out the fulfillment of many *"hidden" keys* and *nuggets of truth* in His Word:

"It is the glory of God to conceal a matter, But the glory of [30]*kings [apostles]* is to search out a matter. *
Proverbs 25:2 (Italics and Parenthesis added)

In the light of this, let us explore some very powerful truths in these two verses of scripture.
- show me Lord.

Ask of Me!
- Here the Lord is saying that we should ask Him to reveal the future movements of His sons. What is it that He has ordained for us? What will we accomplish for and with Him? How will it be accomplished? As the apostolic and prophetic are being fully restored, we should be seeking Him as to what direction they must go. These are all legitimate questions we should be

---

[30] For more teaching on this subject you can read Dr. Roger Sapp's book "The Last Apostles on Earth" – ISBN 1-56043-568-2

asking and seeking answers to.

- He also encourages us to ask Him concerning the work of His hands. Built into the process of asking God, is the deep desire to see the work of His (and not our) hands established. There is a moving first done in His sons in order that we accomplish the greater work of establishing His Kingdom in the earth. The work must first be done in us, before it can be effectively done through us!

You Command Me!

- What an awesome responsibility! God wants us to "command Him"! God has never been reluctant to respond to the confident demands of His people. Moses commanded him "If Your Presence does not go with us then do not move us from this place" Exodus 33:12-23. Jacob declared, "I will not let You go unless You bless me" Genesis 32:22-32. As we seek the face of the Lord and He reveals His plan, for us, and what He wants accomplished, we can confidently and boldly call on him to bring it to pass. It is in this light, that He wants us to "*command Him*".

My hands have created!

- The Lord then goes on to qualify His reason for commanding us to "*ask Him*" and to "*command Him*", by showing that He is more than capable to bring to pass the things that He will show us.

So then, we can truly go *boldly* before the throne of God and call upon Him to bring to pass all that is written in His

Word concerning us - His endtime Church.

We can also typify the Church's journey in the earth similar to the journey that the children of Israel took from Egypt to the Promised Land. The Church came out of *"Egypt"* in 1501 when a German named Martin Luther was mightily used of the Lord to begin the process of restoration. We have gone through the wilderness and have begun final preparations to enter our Promised Land, where we can do the [31]*works of the ministry* in a mature state, as ordained by the Lord, and cause the return of our Lord and King, Jesus Christ. As Joshua took over from Moses and was about to lead the children of Israel into the Promised Land, there was a tremendous requirement on purity.

[32]Let us glean some principles from the Israelites as they journeyed into the Promised Land. We want to use their preparation for entry, as a type of our preparation to enter into God's purpose and destiny for us in this time of apostolic restoration. *grace of preparation a preparation of grace*

After their long forty-year journey from Egypt, which included forty-one encampments in the wilderness, they arrive at the banks of the Jordan River without Moses, the leader and deliverer who took them out of bondage in Egypt.

The Lord then released an apostolic (*sent*) anointing upon Joshua, and commissioned him to lead the people

---

[31] Ephesians 4:12-13
[32] Read Joshua Chapters 1-5

into their God ordained promise.   Today, we are in a similar position as the Lord releases an apostolic anointing upon His Church, in order that we reach our Promised Land of equipping the saints for the work of the ministry.

This apostolic anointing that is being released has the power to cause us to crossover. For too long we have been living on the other side looking and longing to enter into the "*fullness of the measure of the stature of Christ*".

Well, now the time has come for us to possess. However, here are some points to consider as we explore this apostolic grace.

Moses was Dead: Joshua 1:2

In order for the children to enter the Promised Land, Moses had to die. Moses represented the Law, and the Law will not be able to take us into the plans and purposes of the Lord. Legalism is bondage, but wherever the Spirit of the Lord is, there is liberty and Joshua - for his name means, "he will save" - a type of Christ, was chosen to lead the people. Christ came to set us free. This is not a time for dictatorial or manipulative rule.* It is a time for genuine relationships to be built, and for God ordained leadership to be recognized and encouraged.

rightly discerning the Body?

The Apostolic Commissioning And Sending Of Joshua

"After the death of Moses the servant of the LORD, it came to pass that the LORD spoke to Joshua the son of Nun, Moses' assistant, saying: "Moses My servant is dead. Now therefore, arise, go over this Jordan, you and

all this people, to the land which I am giving to them --
the children of Israel. Every place that the sole of your
foot will tread upon I have given you, as I said to
Moses. From the wilderness and this Lebanon as far as
the great river, the River Euphrates, all the land of the
Hittites, and to the Great Sea toward the going down of
the sun, shall be your territory. *No man shall be able to
stand before you all the days of your life; as I was with
Moses, so I will be with you. I will not leave you nor
forsake you.* Be strong and of good courage, for to this
people you shall divide as an inheritance the land which
I swore to their fathers to give them. Only be strong
and very courageous, that you may observe to do
according to all the law which Moses My servant
commanded you; do not turn from it to the right hand
or to the left, that you may prosper wherever you go.
This Book of the Law shall not depart from your
mouth, but you shall meditate in it day and night, that
you may observe to do according to all that is written in
it. For then you will make your way prosperous, and
then you will have good success. Have I not
commanded you? Be strong and of good courage; do
not be afraid, nor be dismayed, for the LORD your God
is with you wherever you go." Joshua 1:1-9 (Italics
added)

God is with us!

What an awesome confidence builder! When God *sends*
us, He never leaves us alone. He confirms His Presence
with every sent one. We can expect the Lord to continue
"showing up" as He did for Joshua and the children of

Israel as they stepped into the Promised Land[33].

Calgary Vision Sept 2005 old train new train

There must be a Change of Mentality

In this particular scenario, Moses their leader of 40 years died and they were transitioning from the old order to a new. That called for a complete change in mindsets. In like manner, what God is doing with us today is a new thing, and so our old wineskins must be destroyed and replaced with new ones. We cannot function under the old order mindset and get the breakthroughs that are needed.

Under the reign of Moses, it was reported that the land could not be taken because giants dwelt there. They also had to contend with the Jordan River, which was at its highest, making it almost impossible to cross over. Without a crossover mentality they would have been stuck.

Every time we are about to enter into the plan and purpose of God there will be major opposition. The devil will always give us reasons why we cannot step into what God wants. Ergo, we must possess a mentality that says to us *"cross over"*.

God is bringing forth a totally new breed of believers who possess the mentality, which says, we can possess the Land. He is making a completely "new wine skin" that can carry this new anointing.

Change Is Constant

We need to understand that in the economy of God there

---

[33] Joshua 1:5

is only one *constant*, and that is *change!* We all must be constantly changing in order to accommodate the dealings and moving of God. Paul describes our lifestyle this way in:

> "But we all, with unveiled face, beholding as in a mirror the glory of the Lord, are being transformed into the same image from glory to glory, just as by the Spirit of the Lord." 2 Corinthians 3:18

The wise man Solomon also saw the progression of the righteous and described it in like manner:

> "But the path of the just is like the shining sun, That shines ever brighter unto the perfect day." Proverbs 4:18

God's description of us!

Throughout scripture the Lord always uses things that we can understand to describe His views and desires for us in relation to His work. For example, at times He declares us to be *His Vineyard*.

His Vineyard

Here the Prophet is describing how the Lord views His church or a local assembly. Isaiah 5:7 identify this:

> "For the vineyard of the LORD of hosts is the house of Israel, And the men of Judah are His pleasant plant."

In order to cultivate or plant a good vineyard (local church) seven things are needed.

- **A fruitful hill had to be located**

- **It had to be dug up and cleared of all stones**

- **A selection process then took place – "and planted the choice vine" in verse 2 suggests that a careful selection process was employed**

→ • **A tower had to be built! Why? You may ask –** In order that watchmen could be set up[34].
  sentinel

- **A winepress (or wine-vat as it was called) also had to be constructed or "hewed out".** By hewing out a hole in the rock, the wine-vat was made. This is where the ripe grapes were crushed in order for wine to be made. This will be dealt with in detail as we study the *wine making process.*

- **A hedge had to be built around the vineyard as indicated by the statement in verse 5 –** This hedge was to act as protection against demonic entities[35].

C. Pierce – the best is yet to come!

→ • **Good expectations! Cultivation must take place with a mindset that the outcome will be an awesome church!**

Wine

Of course the reason why God plants a vineyard is so

---

[34] Isaiah 62:6
[35] Ecclesiastes 10:8

that He can produce wine or allow His Wine (type of the Holy Spirit) to flow through it. In this dimension of wine making we need to understand that God takes us through a process in order that our lives be refined and what we offer to others is of the highest quality.

Wine is also representative of the Holy Spirit, but there is a dimension to which *Wine* is symbolic of our life style.

A process called Vinification makes wine – This is where the ripe grapes are crushed and then placed in a keg to ferment.

Yes, at times it would seem as though we are going through this same process, as the Holy Spirit crushes us and sets us in places of obscurity, to ferment. *The crushed grapes* then go through a process of refinement, where it is poured from vessel to vessel over a period of time and kept in a dark room. It is poured from vessel to vessel in order to get rid of the dregs or lees, which if remains in the wine, will cause it to become bitter.

At times we cry out *"Lord let us out of this place of obscurity, we want to go to the nations, we want to be used more of You Lord."* And instead of Him doing what we perceive as being "used" He pours us into another *"position"* only to be placed in yet another place of obscurity.

In this hour, the Lord wants to ensure that the apostolic ministers that are coming forth have been properly cured. He wants to make sure there are no dregs of bitterness (caused by un-forgiveness, hurt, deception, wrong relationships, etc), so that when they are poured out, the rest of the Body is not contaminated – remember that apostles are being raised up to *equip* God's people for works of service.

The longer it remains and the more it is refined the better the quality. Oh, the refinement process! Even the sinless Messiah had to go through this process! Yes, even Jesus went through His period of obscurity. Remember when He was twelve years old He was the centre of attraction, He held the "spot light" but for a brief moment, as He confounded doctors, lawyers and learned men of His day[36]. However, the next eighteen years of His life were silent, but we read in the book of Hebrews this account of Him:

> "So also Christ did not glorify Himself to become High Priest, but it was He who said to Him: "You are My Son, Today I have begotten You." As He also says in another place: "You are a priest forever according to the order of Melchizedek"; *who, in the days of His flesh, when He had offered up prayers and supplications, with vehement cries and tears* to Him who was able to save Him from death, and was heard because of His godly fear, *though He was a Son, yet He learned obedience by the things which He suffered.* And having been perfected, He became the author of eternal salvation to all who obey Him." Hebrews 5:5-9 (Italics added)

I submit to you that these were Jesus' times of preparation, becoming *"fine wine"* to be poured out for

---

[36] Luke 2: 41-50

the world. When Jesus stepped unto the banks of the Jordan River to be baptized by His cousin John, even though He had not done anything yet for His Father (*no miracles, no preaching, no mighty works*) He declared, "this is My Beloved Son in Whom I am well pleased". God could have made such a declaration, because He knew the process Jesus went through before stepping into His God-ordained destiny.

I declare to you, that Father wants to say the same thing of us if we allow Him by His Holy Spirit to take us through the same process. Do not attempt to come forth before your time, allow the Lord to pour you from vessel to vessel until the refining process is complete, so that when He pours you out there will be no bitter taste. Your ministry will then be of the highest quality.

Before the wine is completed
When the *Vinification* process is completed and the wine is ready for marketing, it is left to stand in the correct amount of light (*too much or too little light affects the quality of the wine*) to end the process, and there you go the wine is ready.

In like manner, when the Lord is ready to use us after carrying us through His "*Vinification process*" He does not release us into the full light all at once. Instead He gradually brings us into our foreordained function to His honour and glory.

The Moab Example[37]

---

[37] Isaiah 15 & 16

- Moab was the son of Lot, a result of incest.[38] Lot had a wrong spirit from the onset[39] unlike Abraham.[40]

- Balak was the king of Moab when he employed Balaam to curse the people of God.[41]

- The men of Israel committed sexual immorality with the women of Moab and God killed 24000.[42]

- God in His mercy had good plans for Moab but he kept messing up – Ruth was a Moabite who ended up in the lineage of Jesus Christ.[43]

Jeremiah 48:11-12

"Moab has been *at ease* from his youth; He *has settled on his dregs, And has not been emptied* from vessel to vessel, *Nor has he gone into captivity.* Therefore *his taste remained in him, And his scent has not changed.* "Therefore behold, the days are coming," says the LORD, "That I shall send him wine-workers Who will tip him over And empty his vessels And break the bottles." (Italics added)

- Maob had been at ease from his youth – from the moment he was born again - he had settled and not changed.

---

[38] Genesis 19:30-38
[39] Genesis 13:5-11
[40] Genesis 18:17-19
[41] Numbers 22:1-20
[42] Numbers 25:1-9
[43] Matthew 1:5

- He had settled on his dregs. - As was shared before, God wants to refine us just as wine is refined, by pouring us from vessel to vessel so that we do not become bitter because of the dregs.

- He had not been emptied from vessel to vessel

- He had not gone into captivity – the process that wine goes through when being refined.

The Lord will often times speak to us in the secret place before we are to publicly make known what He said.[44]

- His taste remained in him – he was bitter (unforgiveness, offences, envy, etc)

- His scent had not changed – as every believer has a particular scent before God. What we do goes up as savour before God – either sweet smelling or offensive.

What is the result of such actions?
"Cursed is he who does the work of the Lord *deceitfully,* and cursed is he who keeps back his sword from blood." Jeremiah 48:10 (Italics added)

Deceitfully – derived from the Hebrew word remiyah – from which we derive the following meanings – Treachery, falsely, full of guile, idly, slack, and slothfully.

Examples:

---

[44] Matthew 10:27

Apate "deceit or deceitfulness" (akin to apatao, "to cheat, deceive, beguile"), that which gives a false impression, whether by appearance, statement or influence.

For example:

- **Riches:**

    "Now he who received seed among the thorns is he who hears the word, and the cares of this world and the deceitfulness of riches choke the word, and he becomes unfruitful." Matthew 13:22

- **Or sin:**

    "Beware, brethren, lest there be in any of you an evil heart of unbelief in departing from the living God; but exhort one another daily, while it is called "Today," lest any of you be hardened through the deceitfulness of sin." Hebrews 3:12-13

- **The Luke 14 Example:**

    "Now when one of those who sat at the table with Him heard these things, he said to Him, "Blessed is he who shall eat bread in the kingdom of God!" Then He said to him, "A certain man gave a great supper and invited many, and sent his servant at supper time to say to those who were invited, 'Come, for all things are now ready.' But they all with one accord began to make excuses. The first said to him, *'I have bought a piece of ground, and I must go and see it.* I ask you to have me excused.' And another said, *'I have bought five yoke of oxen, and I am going to test them.* I ask you to have me excused.' Still another said *'I have married a wife, and therefore I cannot come.'* So that servant came and reported these things to his master. Then the master of the house, being angry, said to his servant, 'Go out quickly into the streets and lanes of the city, and bring in here the poor and the maimed and the lame and the blind.' And the servant said, 'Master, it is done as you commanded, and still there is room.' Then the master said to the servant, 'Go out into the highways and hedges, and compel them to come in, that my house may be filled. For I say to you that none of those men who were invited shall taste my supper.' " Now great multitudes went with Him. And He turned and said to them, If anyone comes to Me and does not *hate* his father and mother, wife and children, brothers and sisters, yes, and his own life also, he cannot be My disciple. And whoever does not bear his cross and come after Me cannot be My disciple. For which of you, intending to build a tower, does not sit down first and count the cost, whether he has enough to finish it-- lest, after he has laid the foundation, and is not able to finish, all who see it begin to mock him, saying, 'This man began to build and was not able to finish.' Or what king, going to make war against another king, does not sit down first and consider whether he is able with ten thousand to meet him who comes against him with twenty thousand? Or else, while the other is still a great way off, he sends a delegation and asks conditions of peace. So likewise, whoever of you does not *forsake all* that he has cannot be My disciple. "Salt is good; but if the salt has lost its flavor, how shall it be seasoned? It is neither fit for the land nor for the dunghill, but men throw it out. He who has ears to hear, let him hear!" Luke 14:15-35 (Italics added)

Lame Excuses

Verse 18 – "I have bought a piece of ground, and I must go and see it. I ask you to have me excused." – *Who buys land before seeing it?*

Verse 19 – "I have bought five yoke of oxen, and I am going to test them. I ask you to have me excused." – *He bought oxen before proving it – what a fool!*

Verse 20 – "I have married a wife, and therefore I cannot come." – *His wife took pre-eminence over work in the Kingdom.*

Jesus' response was that we must hate all else for His Kingdom advance!

Hate is the Greek word *miseo* and carries two shades of meaning to it – In one it translates feelings of resentment or animosity towards a person or thing. Let us examine a few scriptural examples of the usage of the word miseo:

"And you will be *hated* by all for My name's sake. But he who endures to the end will be saved." Matthew 10:22 (Italics added)

"And then many will be offended, will betray one another, and will *hate* one another." Matthew 24:10 (Italics added)

"Blessed are you when men *hate* you, And when they exclude you, And revile you, and cast out your name as evil, For the Son of Man's sake." Luke 6:22 (Italics added)

"Whoever *hates* his brother is a murderer, and you know that no murderer has eternal life abiding in him."
1 John 3:15 (Italics added)

"But to the Son He says: "Your throne, O God, is forever and ever; A sceptre of righteousness is the sceptre of Your Kingdom.   You have loved righteousness and *hated* lawlessness; Therefore God, Your God, has anointed You With the oil of gladness more than Your companions."   Hebrews 1:8-9 (Italics added)

The other translation of miseo but with a different meaning, application and connotation to it, is *"to love less"*. For example:

"If anyone comes to Me and does not *hate* his father and mother, wife and children, brothers and sisters, yes, and his own life also, he cannot be My disciple." Luke 14:26 (Italics added)

Matthew's account of what Jesus said is worded differently, but carries the same meaning. However, as we look at Luke's account in the light of Matthew's, we can see the full use of this word miseo in this particular context:

"He who loves father or mother more than Me is not worthy of Me. And he who loves son or daughter more than Me is not worthy of Me." Matthew 10:37

There is also the Hebrew word *sane'* which is rendered

hate in the following verse of scripture:

> "They *hate* the one who rebukes in the gate, And they abhor the one who speaks uprightly."   Amos 5:10 (Italics added)

The gate represents the place of leadership where justice is to be administered. It is expected that God's leadership will rebuke sin and speak uprightly in those places, fully understanding that they could be hated for it.

However, the worst kind of deception we can get involved in is "*self-deception*", becoming a legend in our own minds. For example:

> "Brethren, if a man is overtaken in any trespass, you who are spiritual restore such a one in a spirit of gentleness, considering yourself lest you also be tempted. Bear one another's burdens, and so fulfill the law of Christ. *For if anyone thinks himself to be something, when he is nothing, he deceives himself.* But let each one examine his own work, and then he will have rejoicing in himself alone, and not in another. For each one shall bear his own load." Galatians 6:1-5 (Italics added)

> "For I say, through the grace given to me, to everyone who is among you, *not to think of himself more highly than he ought to think, but to think soberly*, as God has dealt to each one a measure of faith." Romans 12:3 (Italics added)

"For we dare not class ourselves or compare ourselves with those who commend themselves. But they, measuring themselves by themselves, and comparing themselves among themselves, are not wise. ...*Not boasting* of things beyond measure, that is, *in other men's labors*, but having hope, that as your faith is increased, we shall be greatly enlarged by you in our sphere, to preach the gospel in the regions beyond you, and *not to boast in another man's sphere of accomplishment.* But "he who glories, let him glory in the LORD." For not he who commends himself is approved, but whom the Lord commends." 2 Corinthians 10:12; 15-18 (Italics added)

The Lord was very strong in His choice of words when He described the outcome of anyone who did His work deceitfully – He declared that, that person would be *cursed.*

Cursed is the Hebrew word 'arar' - which means to execrate, accurse, cast out, to denounce as evil or detestable, etc.

Examples:
- Cain:
  "Then the LORD said to Cain, "Where is Abel your brother?" He said, "I do not know. Am I my brother's keeper?" And He said, "What have you done? The voice of your brother's blood cries out to Me from the ground. So now *you are cursed* from the earth, which has opened its mouth to receive your brother's blood from your hand. When you till the ground, it shall no

longer yield its strength to you. A fugitive and a vagabond you shall be on the earth." And Cain said to the LORD, "My punishment is greater than I can bear!" Genesis 4:9-13 (Italics added)

- Christ (*in our place*):
"For as many as are of the works of the law are under the curse; for it is written, "Cursed is everyone who does not continue in all things which are written in the book of the law, to do them."   But that no one is justified by the law in the sight of God is evident, for "the just shall live by faith."   Yet the law is not of faith, but "the man who does them shall live by them." Christ has redeemed us from the curse of the law, having *become a curse for us* (for it is written, "Cursed is everyone who hangs on a tree"), that the blessing of Abraham might come upon the Gentiles in Christ Jesus, that we might receive the promise of the Spirit through faith." Galatians 3:10-14 (Italics added)

That is why Jesus cried out on the cross – "And about the ninth hour *Jesus cried out* with a loud voice, saying, "Eli, Eli, lama sabachthani?" that is, *"My God, My God, why have You forsaken Me?"*   Matthew 27:46 (Italics added)

So let us now paraphrase Jeremiah 48:10
"Anyone who does the work of the Lord falsely, full of guile, idly or slothfully is denounced as evil or detestable, as is anyone who keeps back his or her sword from blood."

Remember what Jesus said:

"Assuredly, I say to you, among those born of women there has not risen one greater than John the Baptist; but he who is least in the kingdom of heaven is greater than he. And *from the days of John the Baptist until now the kingdom of heaven suffers violence, and the violent take it by force.*"   Matthew 11:11-12 (Italics added)

Wineskins – Carriers Of The Anointing!

"No one puts a piece of unshrunk cloth on an old garment; for the patch pulls away from the garment, and the tear is made worse. *Nor do they put new wine into old wineskins, or else the wineskins break, the wine is spilled, and the wineskins are ruined. But they put new wine into new wineskins, and both are preserved.*" Matthew 9:16-17 (Italics added)

The Making of a Wineskin

We dealt with the making of the wine; now let us examine the wineskin.   It is very interesting how a wineskin was made and how it can relate to New Testament experience!

- The animal's head is cut off – representing our mind has to be renewed, so the *"stinking thinking"* has to go.

- The entrails are then removed – representing our beliefs or the things that constitute our lifestyle are removed.

- The skin is then hanged out to dry – representing the Lord making sure that the flesh is completely dead.

- The wine is then poured in and assumes the shape of the wineskin, and then it is capped. When we arrive at this stage; the life that we now have is no longer ours but the new wine that now lives in us – representing a lifestyle of total dependence on the Holy Spirit.

That is why at times you may feel as though your life is being torn apart. Some even begin to question why they believe what they do and launch into a critical analysis of some of their favourite doctrinal positions. Most times it is the work of the Holy Spirit executing the process of making you a new wineskin in order to carry the new anointing He is about to release from the Father! *Hallelujah!*

Sometimes it will seem as though the Lord has forgotten all about you. Take heart, - this is the time He hangs you out to dry, – making sure you are completely dead!

As you stay in that place the Lord will bring you forth – brand new. He will birth in you His Apostolic and Prophetic unction that He is releasing in these last days. *What great news!*

In this hour the Lord is causing His *new wineskins* to take the Church into the next dimension! What a glorious day to be alive! What a time to be connected to the purpose of the Lord!

Chapter 4
Purification For Possessing

After **forty-one** encampments in forty years of wandering in the wilderness, the children of Israel finally came to the place where they were on the brink of crossing over to possess the Promised Land.

When they were about to leave Egypt God did everything through Moses and his spokesman Aaron. Before leaving, they had Passover, which the Lord used as a sign that He would spare the lives of His people when He sent the Destroying Angel. God caused the Egyptians to give up their wealth to the Israelites as a means of the Lord plundering them:

"Now the children of Israel had done according to the word of Moses, and *they had asked from the Egyptians articles of silver, articles of gold, and clothing. And the LORD had given the people favor in the sight of the Egyptians*, so that they granted them what they requested. *Thus they plundered the Egyptians*." Exodus

12:35-36 (Italics added)

The Lord then took them on a journey through the wilderness en route to the Promised Land. However, there was a reason for the Lord taking them through the wilderness for forty years (as there was a much shorter route than the one they took), and it was so that He could prove what was in their hearts:

"And you shall remember that the LORD your God led you all the way these forty years in the wilderness, to humble you and test you, *to know what was in your heart*, whether you would keep His commandments or not." Deuteronomy 8:2 (Italics added)

However, as the children came to the Jordan River and were preparing to cross over, the instructions the Lord gave to Joshua were totally different to the ones He gave Moses:

"Then Joshua rose early in the morning; and they set out from Acacia Grove and came to the Jordan, he and all the children of Israel, and lodged there before they crossed over. So it was, after three days, that the officers went through the camp; and they commanded the people, saying, *"When you see the ark of the covenant of the LORD your God, and the priests, the Levites, bearing it, then you shall set out from your place and go after it. Yet there shall be a space between you and it*, about two thousand cubits by measure. Do not come near it, that you may know the way by which you must go, *for you have not passed*

this way before."   And *Joshua said to the people,*
"Sanctify yourselves, for tomorrow the LORD will do
wonders among you."   Then Joshua spoke to the
priests, saying, "Take up the ark of the covenant and
cross over before the people." So they took up the ark
of the covenant and went before the people." Joshua
3:1-6 (Italics added)

On this occasion instead of Moses (*the Prophet of the
law*) and the rod (*which he used to strike the Rock*) we see
the Ark of the Covenant (*a type of God's Glory*) and the
Priests (*a type of the sanctified believer*) being used. As
we read through the book of Joshua[45], we see some very
relevant and important principles for us today, as we
negotiate this next phase in God's restorative process for
His Church.

Let the Ark (God's Glory and Presence) Go Before
"So it was, after three days, that the officers went
through the camp; and they commanded the people,
saying, "When you see the ark of the covenant of the
LORD your God, and the priests, the Levites, bearing
it, then you shall set out from your place and go after it.
Yet there shall be a space between you and it, about
two thousand cubits by measure. Do not come near it,
that you may know the way by which you must go, for
you have not passed this way before." And Joshua said
to the people, "Sanctify yourselves, for tomorrow the
LORD will do wonders among you."   Then Joshua
spoke to the priests, saying, "Take up the ark of the
covenant and cross over before the people." So they

---

[45] Joshua chapters 3-5

took up the ark of the covenant and went before the people." Joshua 3:3-6

It is absolutely important that we let the *Presence and Glory* of the Lord precede us. Demonic powers are no match for His Presence and Glory.

Under the old order of Moses, it was a *"one-man show"*. When they got to the Red Sea, all that Moses had to do was stretch out his rod, and the waters parted and they went over on dry ground. That was good for that time. Just like the days of the one-man evangelistic crusades, it was good for those days but not in this apostolic time. This time to cross the Jordan, Priests was used. There was a sense of a corporate identity, and not just one man acting.

The Ark Of The Covenant

In the Old Testament the Ark of the Covenant represented the Presence and Glory of God. It essentially contained three articles:

The two tablets of the Law
Aaron's rod that budded
The golden pot of Manna

These three things represented God's Presence with the Israelites.

The Law represented the moral lifestyle He expected from the people.

Aaron's rod that budded represented His divine, delegated authority in the life of the nation of Israel.

The golden pot of Manna represented His divine provision for the people.

A journey through the pages of the Old Testament will reveal that whenever the people of God possessed the Ark, victory would come to them. However, whenever the enemy seized it, they would loose battles.

The Lord commanded Joshua that the priests were to go before the people bearing the Ark of Covenant and when the people saw this, they were to arise and follow the priest. Unlike the parting of the Red Sea under Moses, God used the Priests to carry His Glory in bringing breakthrough and deliverance to His people.

The using of the Priests in taking the people through the Jordan is very significant, and has tremendous relevance to us today, as the Church steps into her age of ultimate conquest.

Today we, the royal priesthood of God, are about to take God's Glory (*which is the revealed Christ*) through the Jordan and into the Land of Promise.

God's Glory
This is not some mystical airy-fairy puff of smoke that rises up into the atmosphere. God's Glory is contained in the revelation of Christ, The Anointed One!

The Bible declares that it is Christ in us which is the

hope of Glory:

> "I now rejoice in my sufferings for you, and fill up in my flesh what is lacking in the afflictions of Christ, for the sake of His body, which is the church, of which I became a minister according to the stewardship from God which was given to me for you, *to fulfill the word of God, the mystery which has been hidden from ages and from generations, but now has been revealed to His saints.* To them *God willed to make known what are the riches of the glory of this mystery* among the Gentiles: *which is Christ in you, the hope of glory.* Him we preach, warning every man and teaching every man in all wisdom, that we may present every man perfect in Christ Jesus.   To this end I also labour, striving according to His working which works in me mightily." Colossians 1:24-29 (Italics added)

When Solomon finished building the Temple to house God's Glory, and was dedicating it, God manifested His Glory because Christ was revealed, as we will see in the issues of the contents of the Ark. This was accentuated by the fact that the Ark of the Covenant was two-thirds empty.

Issues Of The Contents Of The Ark

• The missing golden pot of manna. A very strange and puzzling statement is made:

> "*Nothing was in the ark except the two tablets* which Moses put there at Horeb, when the Lord made a covenant with the children of Israel, when they had come out of Egypt." 2 Chronicles 5:10 (Italics added)

However, the Ark of the Covenant contained more than just the two tablets of the law. A closer look at the book of Hebrews will reveal this:

> "Then indeed, even the first covenant had ordinances of divine service and the earthly sanctuary. For a tabernacle was prepared; the first part, in which was the lampstand, the table, and the showbread, which is called the sanctuary; and behind the second veil, the part of the tabernacle which is called the Holiest of All, which had the golden censer and the ark of the covenant overlaid on all sides with gold, in which were *the golden pot of manna, Aaron's rod that budded, and the tablets of the covenant."* Hebrews 9: 1-4 (Italics added)

Manna represented a type of the revelation of Christ[46] that was given to deal with the issue of murmuring[47]. Murmuring against God-ordained leadership must cease, for the Glory of God to manifest. Part of the technology of the Apostolic gift, is the wisdom to decode the mysteries of God and release it to the Church. This will give the people of God a constant supply of fresh truth, so the murmuring and frustration will cease. This is why there must be a full acceptance of the restoration of Apostles in this hour.

The Ark of the Covenant did not contain the manna, when the glory of God manifested in Solomon's temple, because it was hidden in Christ. Jesus is the true manna[48],

---

[46] John 6:31-33
[47] Exodus 16:1-13, 32
[48] John 6:30-59

but to partake of this manna, which has been hidden from ages and generations, we must be *"Overcomers"*:

"He who has an ear, let him hear what the Spirit says to the churches. To him who *overcomes* I will give some of the *hidden manna to eat.* And I will give him a white stone, and on the stone a new name written which no one knows except him who receives it."' Revelation 2:17 (Italics added)

I prophetically declare to you that the apostolic has the grace and the release from God to take the Church into the *"overcoming"* dimension.

- **The next missing item was Aaron's rod that budded.** This was a type of God's authority. Aaron's rod resulted because of murmuring, fighting for position, and struggle for authority among the Israelites[49]. God then settled the matter in the following way:

"And the Lord spoke to Moses, saying; 'Speak to the children of Israel, and get from them a rod from each father's house, all their leaders according to their fathers' houses – twelve rods. Write each man's name on his rod. 'And you shall write Aaron's name on the rod of Levi. For there shall be one rod for the head of each father's house. 'Then you shall place them in the tabernacle of meeting before the Testimony, where I meet with you. 'And it shall be that *the rod of the man whom I choose will blossom; thus I will rid Myself of*

---

[49] Numbers 16: 1-35

the complaints of the children of Israel, which they make against you.' So Moses spoke to the children of Israel, and each of their leaders gave him a rod apiece, for each leader according to their fathers' houses, twelve rods; and the rod of Aaron was among their rods. And Moses placed the rods before the Lord in the tabernacle of witness. Now it came to pass on the next day that Moses went into the tabernacle of witness, and behold, *the rod of Aaron, of the house of Levi,* had sprouted and put forth buds, *had produced blossoms* and yielded ripe almonds. Then Moses brought out all the rods from before the Lord to all the children of Israel; and they looked, and each man took his rod. And the Lord said to Moses, *'Bring Aaron's rod back before the Testimony, to be kept as a sign against the rebels,* that you may put their complaints away from Me, lest they die.'" Numbers 17:1-10 (Italics added)

The Ark of the Covenant did not contain Aaron's rod when the Glory of God manifested in Solomon's temple, because it was hidden in Christ. All authority is now in Christ and has been delegated to the Church by Him[50]. The glory of God will always be manifested in any place that Jesus Christ is truly Lord, where God-ordained leadership and divine revelation is present.

As **Apostolic Purity** is released, the Church will come to a place where the Glory of God can be manifested. *God hid the revelation of Himself and the issues of authority in Christ.*

---

[50] Matthew 28:18

Jesus promises us that all issues of authority are now in Him. All we need to do is overcome the world, the flesh and the devil, and it's ours. Let us just take a look at some of the promises that the Lord makes for those who overcome:

"He who has an ear let him hear what the Spirit says to the churches. To him who *overcomes* I will give to eat from the tree of life, which is in the midst of the Paradise of God." Revelation 2:7 (Italics added)

"He who has an ear, let him hear what the Spirit says to the churches. To him who *overcomes* I will give some of the *hidden manna* to eat. And I will give him a white stone, and on the stone a new name written which no one knows except him who receives it." Revelation 2:17 (Italics added)

"And he who *overcomes*, and keeps My works until the end, to him I will give *power over the nations*-'He shall rule them with a rod of iron; They shall be dashed to pieces like the potter's vessels.'- as I also have received from My Father; 'and I will give him the morning star. He who has an ear, let him hear what the Spirit says to the churches.'" Revelation 2: 26-29 (Italics added)

"He who *overcomes*, I will make him a pillar in the temple of My God, and he shall go out no more. I will write on him the name of My God and the name of the city of My God, the New Jerusalem, which comes down out of heaven from My God. And I will write on him My new name. He who has an ear, let him hear what the Spirit says to the churches." Revelation 3:12-13 (Italics added)

"To him who *overcomes* I will grant to sit with Me on My throne, *as I also overcame* and sat down with My Father on His throne. He who has an ear, let him hear what the Spirit says to the churches." Revelation 3:21-22 (Italics added)

- **At that time the tablets of the law were the only things present in the Ark.** The two tablets of the law represented the moral code by which the children of Israel lived. They were not removed because they were to act as our schoolmaster until Christ.

"Therefore the law was our tutor to bring us to Christ, that we might be justified by faith. But after faith has come, we are no longer under a tutor." Galatians 3:24

The law is what keeps this world from total decay and chaos; it is the moral agent that convicts people's hearts, thus allowing the Holy Spirit to draw them to Christ.

So as we move deeper into the apostolic restoration, greater strength for *overcoming* is being released in the Church. As the apostles are fully restored to work alongside the prophets, evangelists, pastors and teachers the Church will grow into the fullness of the measure of the stature of Christ, unto a perfect man[51]. This is the most glorious time to be alive, as the Church of Jesus Christ is coming into full maturity. We will see the demonstration

---

[51] Ephesians 4:11-13

of the Power and Glory of God in this season, such as we have never experienced before. With the apostles restored, along with the prophets, evangelists, pastors and teachers, the saints will be thoroughly equipped to do the works of the ministry. *I declare to you that the Glory of God will cover the earth as the waters cover the sea!*

Give the Lord Room or Space

In every move of God, we are to follow Him (we are not to walk alongside Him, or in front of Him) so that we can know the way to go, as we have not passed this way before. However, while this is absolutely true, we need to also understand that even though what God is currently doing maybe new to us, there are basic foundational Christian principles that we are not to neglect. Giving Him room means that we are to walk a safe distance from Him so that we can clearly observe the way in which He is going. This was part of the technology for advancing in the purpose of God in Joshua's time and it is still the same today:

> "So it was, after three days, that the officers went through the camp; and they commanded the people, saying, "When you see the ark of the covenant of the LORD your God, and the priests, the Levites, bearing it, then you shall set out from your place and go after it. Yet there shall be a space between you and it, about two thousand cubits by measure. Do not come near it, that you may know the way by which you must go, for you have not passed this way before." Joshua 3:2-4

Sanctify Yourself

In these times of apostolic restoration we need to walk very lightly, as our pathway is being carved out before us. Let us not crowd the Lord but give Him room. However, right in the midst of Joshua commanding the people to allow the Ark of the Covenant to go before them and not crowd the Lord by leaving a prescribed distance between them and the Lord, he declared:

"...*Sanctify yourselves,* for tomorrow the Lord will do wonders among you." Joshua 3:5 (Italics added)

What an awesome command! Unlike when they were leaving Egypt, when God instituted the Passover, this time He is commanding them to "*Sanctify themselves*". In like manner today there is *a demand from the Spirit of God for Sanctification, Holiness and Purity!* This level of sanctification calls for a complete change in mindsets. What God is doing is a new thing, and our old wineskins must be destroyed and replaced with the new. We cannot function with mindsets of the old order and get the breakthroughs that are needed. *Sanctification, Holiness and Purity* still remains a pre-requisite for the Lord to do *wonders among us!*

In this apostolic age sanctification is going to be a "buzz" word along with other words such as "holiness, purity, righteous living, uprightness, etc... - There is already a demand from the Spirit of God for a *higher level of purity* as the age closes upon us.

There Must Be A Readiness To Hear The Word Of The Lord

"So Joshua said to the children of Israel *"Come here, and hear the words of the Lord your God."* Joshua 3:9 (Italics added)

This is the same Spirit in which Elijah moved in his day - One, which draws us near to God and to His word! Everything that God does, is shaped and crafted by the word He speaks. Jesus proclaimed in Matthew 4:4 "Man shall not live by bread alone, but *by every word that proceeds from the mouth of God*" (Italics added).

The Bible declares that the world in which we live was shaped and crafted by the word of Almighty God. He called forth those things that were not, as though they were. It is no different today; God is shaping and crafting His Church by the word that is going forth from the mouths of His servants. Your life is being shaped by the revelation you are receiving. This is why, there is a requirement upon us to take heed what and how we hear. God is indeed speaking to His people today. To determine to hear God is to determine to obey. This is not the time for rebellion.

The Twelve-Stone Principle

In Joshua chapter four, the Lord commanded that [52]twelve stones be taken from the Jordan, and they were not to be taken by one man but by twelve (representing all the tribes). Again we see the corporate anointing, the spirit

---

[52] Joshua 4:1-20

of unity evident in the apostolic anointing. Twelve is also the number of apostolic government.

However, the reason for the collection of the stones was very important, as they were to be set up in Gilgal as a memorial for the next generation (Gilgal represents the death of unbelief; doubt; scepticism; murmuring and disobedience. It is also the place of the rolling away of reproach and where circumcision takes place). The apostolic anointing that produced this tremendous breakthrough was to be a permanent reminder to all. In this time of apostolic restoration the Church of Jesus Christ will come to a place of *unity and strength* so that the entire world will see and believe that Jesus was indeed *"sent"*.

There is also another powerful point to note regarding these twelve stones that were taken out of the Jordan – it is the place they were to be set up – which was *Gilgal*. I believe that this is one of the things the Spirit of the Lord is doing as He brings us into **Apostolic Purity**.

Gilgal
The stones were to be set up in Gilgal as a memorial for successive generations to know the awesome dealings of a Mighty God! - *Gilgal represents the death of unbelief; doubt; scepticism; murmuring and disobedience.*

• It is also the place of the rolling away of reproach and where circumcision takes place as a memorial for the next generation.

- It was also the place where Agag ([53]*King of the flesh*) was killed. If we were to go back and look at this particular event, it will reveal a dimension of the warfare that takes place for the purposes of God to be fulfilled:

"Then Samuel said, "Bring Agag king of the Amalekites here to me." So Agag came to him cautiously. And Agag said, "Surely the bitterness of death is past." But Samuel said, "As your sword has made women childless, so shall your mother be childless among women." And *Samuel hacked Agag in pieces before the LORD in Gilgal.*" 1 Samuel 15:32-33 (Italics added)

Saul was anointed king over Israel and given a mandate to go and attack and kill all the Amalekites:

"Samuel also said to Saul, "The LORD sent me to anoint you king over His people, over Israel. Now therefore, heed the voice of the words of the LORD. Thus says the LORD of hosts: 'I will punish Amalek for what he did to Israel, how he ambushed him on the way when he came up from Egypt. Now go and attack Amalek, and utterly destroy all that they have, and do not spare them. But kill both man and woman, infant and nursing child, ox and sheep, camel and donkey." 1 Samuel 15:1-3

Please note that a careful study of the word Amalek is

---

[53] See note about this on page 106

translated flesh, making Agag king of the flesh.

Prior to this command from Samuel to Saul to utterly destroy them, these Amalekites attacked and killed some of the Israelites who were on their way to the Promised Land. You might recall the epic battle between them and the Israelites in Rephidim. This was the battle where Joshua led an army against the Amalekites and Aaron and Hur had to hold up Moses' hand, resulting in victory:

the 1st Bible story I distinctly remember 1946? Villencave summer

"Now Amalek came and fought with Israel in Rephidim. And Moses said to Joshua (*deliverer, saviour*), "Choose us some men and go out, fight with Amalek. Tomorrow I will stand on the top of the hill with the rod (*authority*) of God in my hand." So Joshua did as Moses said to him, and fought with Amalek. And Moses, Aaron, and Hur went up to the top of the hill. And so it was, when Moses held up his hand [*a type of the five-fold ministry*], that Israel prevailed; and when he let down his hand, Amalek prevailed. But Moses' hands became heavy; so they took a stone [*a type of the revelation of Christ*] and put it under him, and he sat on it. And Aaron [*priestly ministry*] and Hur [*white linen – a type of the righteousness of the saints*] supported his hands, one on one side, and the other on the other side; and his hands were steady until the going down of the sun. So Joshua defeated Amalek and his people with the edge of the sword. Then the LORD said to Moses, "*Write this for a memorial in the book and recount it in the hearing of Joshua, that I will utterly blot out the remembrance of Amalek from under heaven.*" And Moses built an altar and called its name, The-Lord-Is-

My-Banner; for he said, *"Because the LORD has sworn: the LORD will have war with Amalek from generation to generation."* Exodus 17:8-16 (Italics and Parenthesis added)

In this hour, God by His Spirit is raising up a Joshua company with His King-Priest anointing fueled by divine revelation from His *five-fold* ministers who are walking in purity and ministering from that place. However, Saul, without a sense of history and relevance to previous moves of God, disobeyed the word of the Lord and spared Agag, king of the Amalekites and the best of the flock.

He also, being very religious, thought he could get away with the infamous punch line - *"we did it to sacrifice to the Lord"* - to which the Prophet responded:

"Has the LORD as great delight in burnt offerings and sacrifices, As in obeying the voice of the LORD? Behold, *to obey is better than sacrifice*, And to heed than the fat of rams. For rebellion is as the sin of witchcraft, And stubbornness is as iniquity and idolatry." 1 Samuel 15:22-23 (Italics added)

Similarly today, God by His Holy Spirit is at war against the flesh. He wants the flesh destroyed; nothing must be spared no matter how "good" it may seem to us. Agag, king of the flesh *must* be destroyed.

I proclaim to you by the Spirit of Almighty God, this is your moment of breakthrough, this is the time to arise from where you are, allow the Lord to give you a

fresh change of clothing so that you may continue the journey. God requires purity in these final days and it doesn't matter where you have been or what you have done, obey the voice of the Lord and repent, get up from where you have fallen and re-enter the race, redeem the lost time! I know some of you reading this book are in that place, but as I write I hear the Spirit of the Lord saying Grace has been released so that you can in fact return to your first love. He says He can re-ignite the passion and hunger you once had; He can breathe on the coals of your life and let His fire burn once again if you will only ask Him to. Oh, hear me, this is the season to change; this is the season to be holy, pure and righteous. Grace is being poured out for us to overcome! God has released His sending (Apostolic) Spirit into His Church and like He did with Isaiah, He can do with you if you confess like Isaiah did – I am a man/woman of unclean lips, but I want to be sent, I want the apostolic grace to function in my life – and the Lord took a burning coal and touched his mouth and cleansed him.

• It was also a part of Samuel's Prophetic circuit when he judged Israel[54]

• It was the place where "manna" *(what is it?)* ceased[55] and they entered into food of the Promised Land – which is abundance!

---

[54] 1 Samuel 7:15-16
[55] Joshua 5:10-12

The "So That" Principle

"Then he spoke to the children of Israel, saying: "When your children ask their fathers in time to come, saying, 'What are these stones?' "then you shall let your children know, saying, 'Israel crossed over this Jordan on dry land'; for the LORD your God dried up the waters of the Jordan before you until you had crossed over, as the LORD your God did to the Red Sea, which He dried up before us until we had crossed over, *that all the peoples of the earth may know the hand of the LORD, that it is mighty, that you may fear the LORD your God forever.*" Joshua 4:21-24 (Italics added)

Please understand, that in everything God does there is the *"so that"* dimension to keep things in their proper perspective. The reason why God is doing all that He is today, in restoring apostles and causing the five-fold ministry gifts to be manifested, is *"so that"* He can bring His Church to a place of maturity and strength, in order for His Glory to be shown forth from His Church into the earth.

He is not restoring apostles today to tickle someone's ego or to merely give someone a title or an exalted position of authority – No! He is totally interested in His Church, the Bride of Christ maturing in every aspect of the Christ-Like nature. Ephesians chapter 4 still rings true in every sector of His Church:

"And He Himself gave some to be Apostles, some Prophets, some evangelists, and some pastors and teachers, for the equipping of the saints for the work of ministry, *for the* edifying of the body of Christ, till we all come to the unity of the faith and of the knowledge of the Son of God, to a perfect man, to the measure of the stature of the fullness of Christ; *that* we should no longer be children, tossed to and fro and carried about with every wind of doctrine, by the trickery of men, in the cunning craftiness of deceitful plotting, but, speaking the truth in love, may grow up in all things into Him who is the head--Christ--from whom the whole body, joined and knit together by what every joint supplies, according to the effective working by which every part does its share, *causes* growth of the body for the edifying of itself in love.   This I say, therefore, and testify in the Lord, that you should no longer walk as the rest of the Gentiles walk, in the futility of their mind, having their understanding darkened, being alienated from the life of God, because of the ignorance that is in them, because of the hardening of their heart; who, being past feeling, have given themselves over to lewdness, to work all uncleanness with greediness.   But you have not so learned Christ, if indeed you have heard Him and have been taught by Him, as the truth is in Jesus: *that you put off,* concerning your former conduct, the old man which grows corrupt according to the deceitful lusts, and be renewed in the spirit of your mind, and *that you put on* the new man which was created according to God, in *true righteousness and holiness.*"   Ephesians 4:11-24 (Italics added)

Chapter 5
Kings And Priests

The Kingly-Priesthood Of The Believer

The visible priesthood in the nation of Israel began with Aaron, a Levite, who was Moses' older brother. - (Please understand that in *Melchizedek* the priesthood existed long before Aaron was appointed). As a matter of fact, he was the first high priest. His training in becoming high priest involved several years in Egypt as the God-ordained spokesman for Moses, when the Lord delivered His people from bondage:

"Now take Aaron your brother, and his sons with him, from among the children of Israel, that he may minister to Me as priest, Aaron and Aaron's sons: Nadab, Abihu, Eleazar, and Ithamar. And you shall make *holy garments* for Aaron your brother, for glory and for beauty. So you shall speak to all who are gifted artisans, whom I have filled with the spirit of wisdom, that they may make Aaron's garments, *to consecrate him, that he may minister to Me as priest.* And these are the garments, which they shall make: a breastplate, an ephod, a robe, a skilfully woven tunic, a turban, and a sash. So they shall make *holy garments* for Aaron your brother and his sons, *that he may minister to Me as priest."* Exodus 28:1-4 (Italics added)

One of the highlights of his function as High Priest was to go into the Holy of Holies once a year (the Day of Atonement) with the blood of bulls and goats to make reparation for the priesthood and the Israelites. Aaron had four sons, and at his death, his priestly garments and office were transferred to his oldest living son, Eleazar so that the priesthood could continue. However, please understand that no matter how well Aaron and the succeeding priests did their job, that priesthood was imperfect.

In the New Testament the priesthood changed and a new beginning was implemented, as we see Jesus Christ becoming the great High Priest after the order of *Melchizedek*:

"For *every high priest taken from among men is appointed for men in things pertaining to God*, that he may offer both gifts and sacrifices for sins. He can have compassion on those who are ignorant and going astray, since he himself is also beset by weakness. Because of this he is required as for the people, so also for himself, to offer sacrifices for sins. *And no man takes this honor to himself, but he who is called by God, just as Aaron was. So also Christ did not glorify Himself to become High Priest, but it was He who said to Him*: "You are My Son, Today I have begotten You." As He also says in another place: *"You are a priest forever According to the order of Melchizedek*"; who, in the days of His flesh, when He had offered up prayers and supplications, with vehement cries and tears to Him who was able to save Him from death, and was heard because of His godly fear, though He was a Son, yet He learned obedience by the things which He suffered. He became the author of eternal salvation to all who obey Him, *called by God as High Priest "according to the order of Melchizedek."*   Hebrews 5:1-11 (Italics added)

A Brief Note On Melchizedek

Melchizedek is translated "*king of righteousness*". He was the king of Salem (known as Jerusalem) and "a priest of The Most High God," who went out to congratulate Abraham on his victory over Chedorlaomer and his allies. Melchizedek brought bread and wine (a type of Covenant Supper) for, and bestowed his blessing upon Abraham. In return Abraham gave to Melchizedek -the royal priest of The Most High God- a tenth of all the substance they had taken from the enemy:

"And the king of Sodom went out to meet him at the Valley of Shaveh (that is, the King's Valley), after his return from the defeat of Chedorlaomer and the kings who were with him. Then Melchizedek king of Salem brought out bread and wine; he was the priest of God Most High. And he blessed him and said: "Blessed be Abram of God Most High, Possessor of heaven and earth; And blessed be God Most High, Who has delivered your enemies into your hand." And he gave him a tithe of all." Genesis 14:17-20

The relation between Melchizedek and Christ as type and antitype is made in the epistle to the Hebrews to consist in the following: each was a priest (1) who is not of the Levitical tribe; (2) who is superior to Abraham; (3) whose beginning and end are unknown; (4) who is not only a priest but also a king of righteousness and peace. "Without father," etc. (Hebrews 7:3), refers to priestly genealogies. Melchizedek is not found on the register of the only line of legitimate priests; his father's name is not recorded, nor his mother's; no evidence points out his line of descent from Aaron. It is not affirmed that he had no father or that he was not born at any time or died on any day; but these facts were nowhere found on the register of the Levitical priesthood. Melchizedek offers an expressive type of Christ, the *King-Priest*, especially of the Messiah's work in resurrection, inasmuch as the ancient character offers bread and wine, memorials of sacrifice. The writer to the Hebrews beautifully describes the everlasting continuance and *kingly authority of Christ's high priesthood* by the phrase "according to the order of Melchizedek":

"This hope we have as an anchor of the soul, both sure and steadfast, and which enters the Presence behind the veil, where the forerunner has entered for us, *even Jesus, having become High Priest forever according to the order of Melchizedek.*" Hebrews 6:19-20 (Italics added) "And inasmuch as He was not made priest without an oath (for they have become priests without an oath, but He with an oath by Him who said to Him: "*The LORD has sworn* And will not relent, "*You are a priest forever According to the order of Melchizedek*"), by so much more Jesus has become a surety of a better covenant. Also there were many priests, because they were prevented by death from continuing. But He, because *He continues forever, has an unchangeable priesthood.*" Hebrews 7:20-24 (Italics added)

The priesthood, as handed down through the line of Aaron, was often set aside by death. The Melchizedek aspect of Christ's priesthood portrays Christ in the perpetuity of His priestly office. "He always lives to make intercession" (Hebrews 7:25). Although the Aaronic priesthood could typify Christ's priestly work, it was limited in portraying the full scope of His priestly ministry. The Melchizedek type supplements the Aaronic type. As "king of righteousness" and "king of peace" Melchizedek is introduced "without father, without mother, without descent" being recorded, whereas this was an essential in the Aaronic priesthood (see Ezra 2:62-63; Exodus 29:9, 29-30; Leviticus 21:13-14). This is a second peculiarity of the Messiah's priesthood, that it is not derived from another before Him, and "passeth not to another" after Him (Hebrews 7:24). The "without father, without mother, without genealogy, having neither beginning of days nor end of life, but made like the Son of God, remains a priest continually" (Hebrews 7:3), refers to Melchizedek officially, not naturally. Melchizedek was without father, etc., i.e. sacerdotally he was independent of his descent, unlike the Aaronic priests, who forfeited the priesthood if they could not trace their descent; for example:

"These sought their listing among those who were registered by genealogy, but it was not found; therefore they were excluded from the priesthood as defiled. And the governor said to them that they should not eat of the most holy things till a priest could consult with the Urim and Thummim." Nehemiah 7: 64-65

Melchizedek had no fixed beginning or end of his kingly priesthood, such as the Levitical priests, who began at 30 and ended at 50 years of age.

Christ as man had "father, mother, beginning of days and end of life, and descent" genealogically traced (Hebrews 7:3). Melchizedek therefore cannot have been absolutely without these; but officially he was without them, even as the antitypical priest Messiah was officially and sacerdotally without them. Messiah was not of Levi, but of Judah, so did not receive His priesthood by inheritance.

Doubtless Melchizedek had father and mother by birth, but as king priest, had neither predecessor nor successor. The Aaronic priesthood was local, temporary, and national; the Melchizedek priesthood was prior to the Levitical temporary law, and so worldwide and everlasting. The Aaronic high priest claimed no authority over other nations. Melchizedek was priest not only to his own city Salem, but is recognized as such by Abram the representative of God's church and people; and the king of Sodom tacitly acquiesces in this claim to an universal priesthood. This is the significance of the title, priest of "the Possessor of heaven and earth." Melchizedek is the first and the last who by God's appointment, and in God's name, exercised the priesthood for Shemite and Hamite alike, the forerunner of gospel universality which joins under Christ all of every race (Galatians 3:28; Colossians 3:11; Romans 10:12). Melchizedek was superior to Abram, in that he blessed and received tithes from him (the giver's token of acknowledgment that all his property is God's), and so was superior to Levi and the Aaronic priesthood, which were in Abram's loins.[56]

The Royal Priesthood

This Royal (kingly/apostolic) Priesthood is now applied to the Christian.   The Aaronic priesthood also typifies the New Testament "Royal Priesthood" of Jesus Christ as is highlighted in the following verses:

"Coming to Him as to a living stone, rejected indeed by men, but chosen by God and precious, you also, as living stones, are being built up a spiritual house, *a holy priesthood*, to offer up spiritual sacrifices acceptable to God through Jesus Christ.   ...But you are a chosen generation, *a royal priesthood, a holy nation*, His own special people, that you may proclaim the praises of Him who called you out of darkness into His marvellous light..." 1 Peter 2:4-5; 9 (Italics added)

This same understanding is also revealed in the book of Revelation:

"And has *made us kings and priests* to His God and Father, to Him be glory and dominion forever and ever Amen." Revelation 1:6   (Italics added)

---

[56] * Taken from Fausset's Bible Dictionary and Used by permission from Biblesoft (PCSB Version 3)

"And have made us kings and priests to our God; And we shall reign on the earth." Revelation 5:10

This Royal (kingly/apostolic) Priesthood is not a new concept, as the Lord made reference or pointed to it in Melchizedek - combining kingship with the priesthood. He was both king of Salem and priest of God.[57] This was always in the heart of God - having a Kingdom of Priests or Royal Priesthood. He re-emphasised it even before Aaron was established as High Priest over the nation of Israel. He spoke His heart to Moses and declared:

"And Moses went up to God, and the LORD called to him from the mountain, saying, "Thus you shall say to the house of Jacob, and tell the children of Israel: 'You have seen what I did to the Egyptians, and how I bore you on eagles' wings and brought you to Myself. Now therefore, *if you will indeed obey My voice and keep My covenant*, then you shall be a special treasure to Me above all people; for all the earth is Mine. And *you shall be to Me a kingdom of priests and a holy nation.*' These are the words which you shall speak to the children of Israel." Exodus 19:3-6 (Italics added)

This same Royal Priesthood was demonstrated in the anointing of Joshua the high priest in the following:

"Then the word of the LORD came to me, saying: "Receive the gift from the captives--from Heldai, Tobijah, and Jedaiah, who have come from Babylon—

---

[57] Genesis 14:11

and go the same day and enter the house of Josiah the son of Zephaniah. *Take the silver and gold, make an elaborate crown, and set it on the head of Joshua* the son of Jehozadak, *the high priest.* Then speak to him, saying, 'Thus says the LORD of hosts, saying: "Behold, the Man whose name is the BRANCH! From His place He shall branch out, And He shall build the temple of the LORD; Yes, He shall build the temple of the LORD. He shall bear the glory, And shall sit and rule on His throne; So *He shall be a priest on His throne*, And the counsel of peace shall be between them both." "Now the elaborate crown shall be for a memorial in the temple of the LORD for Helem, Tobijah, Jedaiah, and Hen the son of Zephaniah. Even those who are far away shall come and build the temple of the LORD. Then you shall know that the LORD of hosts has sent Me to you. *And this shall come to pass if you diligently obey the voice of the LORD your God.*" Zechariah 6:9-15 (Italics added)

Remember that Jesus Christ, our Heavenly Aaron, the Head of His body the Church, has entered into the heavens as a Forerunner after the order of Melchizedek, and the same king-priest anointing that is upon our Heavenly Aaron is flowing down upon His Body, the Church.

Chapter 6 – Part I
Qualifications And
Blemishes Of The Priesthood
I

In **this**, and the following two chapters, we will explore the initial qualifications of the Aaronic priesthood and translate them into New Testament reality.

When the Lord was instituting the Aaronic priesthood He established certain criteria for smooth and proper functioning. The following portion gives the general, foundational outline for the priesthood, which we will be exploring:

"And the LORD spoke to Moses, saying, "Speak to Aaron, saying: 'No man of your descendants in succeeding generations, who has any defect, may approach to offer the bread of his God. For *any man who has a defect shall not approach*: a man *blind or lame*, who has a *marred face or any limb too long*, a man who has a *broken foot or broken hand, or is a hun-*

chback or a dwarf, or a man who has a *defect in his eye, or eczema or scab, or is a eunuch.* No man of the descendants of Aaron the priest, who has a defect, shall come near to offer the offerings made by fire to the LORD. He has a defect; he shall not come near to offer the bread of his God. *He may eat the bread of his God, both the most holy and the holy; only he shall not go near the veil or approach the altar, because he has a defect, lest he profane My sanctuaries; for I the LORD sanctify them.'"* Leviticus 21:16-23 (Italics added)

There are many significant principles outlined in this passage of scripture that we need to extract as we move deeper into this time of apostolic restoration. The Lord is setting the stage for an incredible time of harvest for His Church and we need to be prepared.

In the study of scriptures there is a principle, which is known as the "first mention principle" or "law of first mention" – This is a principle by which the interpretation of any verse is aided by considering the first time its subject appears in Scripture. In general, the first time a thing is mentioned in Scripture it carries with it a meaning, which will be consistent throughout the entire Bible. In the light of this we will look at the qualifications for the priesthood as described in *Leviticus 21: 16-23* in the next chapter.

Please understand that God's standards are still very high, however, the one major difference between the Old and New Testaments is that while the Old demanded righteousness, it could not provide for it – in that even though the High Priest would make atonement for the sins of the people, he would also have to do it for himself and that had to be done every year – on the other hand the New demands righteousness and holiness (without which no one will see God – Hebrews 12:14-15) and provision has been made for it through the once and for all *"perfect sacrifice"* of the Lamb that was slain – Christ Jesus – our Heavenly High Priest after the Order of Melchizedek!

The only manifestation of Christ that the earth will ever see before the second coming of Jesus is through His Church. Whatever representation of Christ the Church gives to the world that is all they will have. Now this is very vital and extremely important because salvation can come through no other but Jesus. You see the Church has to rise to a new level of relevance in the earth before Jesus' return. I was listening to excerpts from a message preached by Apostle Anderson Williams of the World Breakthrough Network, Trinidad, West Indies, and he made a very salient point, which I would like to bring to light. He typified man as an icon on a desktop of a computer. For example on your windows desktop there might be an icon or shortcut for the word processor, and once you double click on that icon it will open up the real program. Now the icon is not the program, but is connected to and represents the program. *In like manner* when the world double clicks on the Christian (who can be identified as an icon or shortcut to Christ) the real Christ should manifest.

[58]Ezekiel the Prophet declared that God sought for a

---

[58] Ezekiel 22:30

man to make up the wall and to stand in the gap because the state of the nation was deplorable.   There was downright unrighteous, unholy living that was detestable in the sight of the Lord, and He wanted the situation corrected. As we read through the chapter we can see how easy it is for us to refer to it as the day and age in which we live – Leadership (represented by prophets, priests and princes or officials) was in total chaos, there was a blurring of the lines between the holy and the profane, there was *merchandizing of the anointing and gifting* and the list goes on, very similar to what we are witnessing today. And it is in the midst of that level of chaos the Lord sought and is seeking for a man to bring order.

The man that the Lord is raising up in this hour is a many-membered apostolic man who will walk in purity and holiness, who will not *merchandize the anointing*, who will stir the Church into new levels of function before the Lord.   One, who will ensure, that the Church of Jesus Christ never cascades into chaos and despair again.   This man is already emerging in the earth! Many refer to him as the *Man-Child* of Revelation 5:12 who the Lord will raise up with an anointing to rule the nations in direct opposition to entrenched demonic forces. Hallelujah!

Merchandizing Of The Anointing And Gifting
The word merchandize is translated from several Hebrew and Greek words such as the following:

Hebrew
Cachar - it is from a root meaning "*to travel around as a peddler*"; and is translated thus in:

"Thus says the LORD: "The labour of Egypt and *merchandise* of Cush And of the Sabeans, men of stature, Shall come over to you, and they shall be yours…" Isaiah 45:14 (Italics added)

Rekhullah, is from a root meaning "*to travel for trading purposes*"; and is translated thus in:

"They will plunder your riches and pillage your *merchandise*; they will break down your walls and destroy your pleasant houses; they will lay your stones, your timber, and your soil in the midst of the water." Ezekiel 26:12 (Italics added)

Ma`arabh, is from a root meaning "*to intermix, to barter*"; and is translated thus in:

"Elders of Gebal and its wise men Were in you to caulk your seams; All the ships of the sea And their oarsmen were in you To market your *merchandise*." Ezekiel 27:9 (Italics added)

"Your riches, wares, and *merchandise*, Your mariners and pilots, Your caulkers and merchandisers, All your men of war who are in you, And the entire company which is in your midst, Will fall into the midst of the seas on the day of your ruin." Ezekiel 27:27 (Italics added)

"When your wares went out by sea, You satisfied many people; You enriched the kings of the earth With your many luxury goods and your *merchandise*. But you are broken by the seas in the depths of the waters; Your *merchandise* and the entire company will fall in your midst." Ezekiel 27:33-34 (Italics added)

Amar, translated in the King James Version as "*make merchandise of*," but in the Revised Version (British and American) "*deal with as a slave*," or the Revised Version margin "*deal with as a chattel*", in the following verses:

"And it shall be, if thou have no delight in her, then thou shalt let her go whither she will; but thou shalt not sell her at all for money, thou shalt not make *merchandise* of her, because thou hast humbled her." Deuteronomy 21:14 *KJV* (Italics added)

"If a man be found stealing any of his brethren of the children of Israel, and maketh *merchandise* of him, or selleth him; then that thief shall die; and thou shalt put evil away from among you." Deuteronomy 24:7 *KJV* (Italics added)

"Then, if you have no delight in her, you shall let her go where she will; but *you shall not sell her for money, you shall not treat her as a slave*, since you have humiliated her." Deuteronomy 21:14 *RSV* (Italics added)

"If a man is found stealing one of his brethren, the people of Israel, and if he *treats him as a slave or sells him*, then that thief shall die; so you shall purge the evil from the midst of you." Deuteronomy 24:7 *RSV* (Italics added)

This is very interesting as this is exactly how the Lord views those who trade in the anointing. Some ministries use people with the anointing as slaves, and merchandize them. The Apostle Peter in his admonition echoes this same concept, as we study the Greek words:

Greek
Emporion - is from a root meaning to "*make merchandise of you*" - treat you like a slave, as is used in:

"But there arose false prophets also among the people, as among you also there shall be false teachers, who shall privily bring in destructive heresies, denying even the Master that bought them, bringing upon themselves swift destruction. And many shall follow their lascivious doings; by reason of whom the way of the truth shall be evil spoken of. And in covetousness shall they *with feigned words make merchandise of you*: whose sentence now from of old lingereth not, and their destruction slumbereth not." 2 Peter 2: 1-3 (Italics added) *ASV*

Remember Simon the sorcerer in the book of Acts:

"But there was a certain *man called Simon*, who previously *practiced sorcery* in the city and astonished the people of Samaria, claiming that he was someone great, to whom they all gave heed, from the least to the greatest, saying, "This man is the great power of God." And they heeded him because he had astonished them with his sorceries for a long time. But when they believed Philip as he preached the things concerning the kingdom of God and the name of Jesus Christ, both men and women were baptized. *Then Simon himself also believed; and when he was baptized he continued with Philip, and was amazed, seeing the miracles and signs which were done.* Now *when the apostles* who were at Jerusalem heard that Samaria had received the word of God, they sent Peter and John to them, who, when they had come down, *prayed for them that they might receive the Holy Spirit.* For as yet He had fallen upon none of them. They had only been baptized in the name of the Lord Jesus. Then *they laid hands on them, and they received the Holy Spirit.* And *when Simon saw* that through the laying on of the apostles' hands the Holy Spirit was given, *he offered them money, saying, "Give me this power also, that anyone on whom I lay hands may receive the Holy Spirit." But Peter said to him, "Your money perish with you, because you thought that the gift of God could be purchased with money!* You have neither part nor portion in this matter, for *your heart is not right in the sight of God.* Repent therefore of this your wickedness, and pray God if perhaps the thought of your heart may be forgiven you. For I see that *you are poisoned by bitterness and bound by iniquity."* Acts 8: 9-23 (Italics added)

Simon was operating under a false apostolic authority (probably some kind of mind control), and bewitched the people. He moved in some false, demonic signs and the people feared him. However, when the Kingdom of God was preached, the demonic powers were broken and the eyes of the people were opened and they gladly received the word and were baptized.

Phillip being an Evangelist needed apostolic grace and impartation to take the people into the next level and as soon as Apostles Peter and John arrived, true miracles, signs and wonders were witnessed for the first time, including a visible, manifested, evidence of several persons receiving the Holy Spirit through the laying on of the Apostles' hands.

At that point Simon tried merchandizing the apostolic anointing and Peter rose up in true **Apostolic Purity** and rebuked him, even though the word of God stated that this man also believed and was baptized.

This is still being done today as many traffic in the anointing.   However, this true apostolic dimension is returning to the Body of Christ as the Holy Spirit restores apostles who will function in purity and not *merchandize* the anointing.

Jesus used the very same word *"Emporion"* when He encountered the traffickers in the temple in:

"And he found in the temple those that sold oxen and sheep and doves, and the changers of money sitting: and he made a scourge of cords, and cast all out of the temple, both the sheep and the oxen; and he poured out the changers' money, and overthrew their tables; and to them that sold the doves he said, Take these things hence; *make not my Father's house a house of merchandise.*" John 2: 14-16 (Italics added) *ASV*

Jesus is still doing this very thing today in His temple, the Church, as there are many who continue in this devious practice of merchandizing God's people. There are many that barter and trade the anointing such as they will not go and preach the word of God if "*the price is not right*". Let me make myself clear here. I know we are not to muzzle the ox that treads out the grain and the workman is indeed worthy of his wages etc. However, we need to understand that if we are to walk in the levels of purity that is being required in this hour, we have to leave our wages wholly up to the Holy Spirit. Let Him establish what we should or should not get, and let us get on with business at hand, which is to assist in bringing the Church to a place of predestined maturity and greatness in the earth.

The apostle Paul in writing to the Corinthian church in 2 Corinthians 2: 17 declared:

"For we are not, as so many, *peddling* the word of God; but as of sincerity, but as from God, we speak in the sight of God in Christ." (Italics added)

Here the word used for peddling is the Greek word *kapeeleuontes* and it conveys the idea of those who sit in the marketplace buying and selling. This word also speaks of dealers in victuals and all sorts of wares, but was especially applied to retailers of wine, with whom adulteration and short measure were matters of course.

The moral application of this word was familiar in Classical Greek. Lucian says: "The philosophers deal out their instructions like hucksters." Plato: "Those who carry about the wares of knowledge, and make the rounds of the cities, and sell or retail them to any customer who is in want of them, praise them all alike; though I should not wonder if many of them were really ignorant of their effect upon the soul; and their customers equally ignorant, unless he who buys of them happens to be a physician of the soul" (Protagoras, 313).

We have to be so careful as to not blur the lines where this is concerned. I urge those called to the apostolic office to walk pure in this area. Remember Judas (the one who carried the money bag), who sold out Jesus and lost his place amongst the *"Twelve Apostles of the Lamb"* - an awesome, powerful designation. If he who actually walked with Jesus did it, apostles and ministers today are not without temptation. Also, it will do well for us to understand that one of the reasons that Lucifer was cast out of heaven was because of his *merchandizing* as was attested to in the following scriptural text:

"Thou wast perfect in thy ways from the day that thou wast created, till iniquity was found in thee. By the *multitude of thy merchandise* they have filled the midst of thee with violence, and thou hast sinned: therefore I will cast thee as profane out of the mountain of God: and I will destroy thee, O covering cherub, from the midst of the stones of fire. Thine heart was lifted up because of thy beauty, thou hast corrupted thy wisdom by reason of thy brightness: I will cast thee to the ground, I will lay thee before kings, that they may behold thee. Thou hast defiled thy sanctuaries by the multitude of thine iniquities, *by the iniquity of thy traffick*; therefore will I bring forth a fire from the midst of thee, it shall devour thee, and I will bring thee to ashes upon the earth in the sight of all them that behold thee." *KJV* Ezekiel 28:15-18 (Italics added)

"You were perfect in your ways from the day you were created, Till iniquity was found in you. "By *the abundance of your trading* you became filled with violence within, And you sinned; Therefore I cast you as a profane thing Out of the mountain of God; And I destroyed you, O covering cherub, From the midst of the fiery stones. "Your heart was lifted up because of your beauty; You corrupted your wisdom for the sake of your splendour; I cast you to the ground, I laid you before kings, That they might gaze at you. "You defiled your sanctuaries By the multitude of your iniquities, By *the iniquity of your trading*; Therefore I brought fire from your midst; It devoured you, And I turned you to ashes upon the earth In the sight of all who saw you." Ezekiel 28:15-18 (Italics added)

[59]Wealth is one of the pillars of the apostolic and we will do well to understand that this wealth is not for individual ministers or ministries to exploit, but to be used in advancing God's Kingdom in the earth.

In this hour the Lord is calling us to be like the sons of *Zadok*, an exemplary *high priest*.

---

[59] You can read the author's book "Five Pillars of The Apostolic" for a more in-depth analysis of this pillar of the Apostolic.

Reviewing The Zadok Anointing

As we read through the book of Ezekiel from *chapter forty to chapter forty-eight*, what was being described was a new city and temple that the Lord was showing to Ezekiel. It is described today as *"Ezekiel's Temple"*. However, as we study these chapters we need to note that Ezekiel's restored temple is not a blueprint, but a vision that stresses the purity and spiritual vitality of the ideal place of worship and those who will worship there. It is not intended for an earthly, physical fulfillment, but expresses the truth found in the name of the new city - *"THE LORD IS THERE"*[60]. This speaks to us of an end-time church that is completely sold out to the kingdom of God, where God Himself will dwell.

In chapter forty-four we see the Lord establishing those who will be admitted to the temple from verses 1-9, and then He goes on in verses 10-31, to describe the quality of the priesthood and laws that would govern them. Here we see two categories of priests; [61]one group who will only minister before the people; and the other group, *"the sons of Zadok"*[62] who will minister both before the Lord and before the people.

In this time of apostolic restoration, God is going to bring a separation in the ranks of professing Christianity.

We want to take a closer look at Zadok and the sons of Zadok. If we were to take a look at the listings of David's

---

[60] Ezekiel 48:35
[61] Ezekiel 44: 10-14
[62] Ezekiel 44: 15-31

rulers in 2 Samuel 8:17, we will find the name of Zadok, a young priest who was a descendant of Aaron, as recorded in 1 Chronicles 6:12 & 49-53. This priest was under Saul but had to brave the reproach of being a heretic and a traitor when he left Saul (a type of the religious system of man) to join David (God's ordained government; a type of the apostolic/prophetic). As a matter of fact, that was a very wise move in his time, for Saul had ordered Doeg to slaughter the 85 priests of the Lord who remained with Saul:

> "And the king said, "You shall surely die, Ahimelech, you and all your father's house!" Then the king said to the guards who stood about him, "Turn and kill the priests of the LORD, because their hand also is with David, and because they knew when he fled and did not tell it to me." But the servants of the king would not lift their hands to strike the priests of the LORD. And the king said to Doeg, "You turn and kill the priests!" So Doeg the Edomite turned and struck the priests, and killed on that day eighty-five men who wore a linen ephod. Also Nob, the city of the priests, he struck with the edge of the sword, both men and women, children and nursing infants, oxen and donkeys and sheep--with the edge of the sword. Now one of the sons of Ahimelech the son of Ahitub, named Abiathar, escaped and fled after David. And Abiathar told David that Saul had killed the LORD's priests." 1 Samuel 22:16-21

He also commanded the destruction of the city of Nob, which was the city of the priests. Had he not decided to go with David, Zadok would have been a dead man.

Zadok then can represent anyone who is willing to leave the old order and religious traditions behind and step into what God, by His Spirit, is doing in this hour - those who are willing to suffer the reproach of their peers and step outside the *"camp"*[63] to fulfill the will of God. It is a new breed of believers that will follow David (a type of the apostolic/prophetic restoration that is bringing reformation to the Church) - A new breed that will cause their "sons and daughters" to continue the forward, progressive flow under the Davidic anointing.

Another interesting account in the life of this awesome high priest is found in 2 Samuel 15. Saul had already died and David had ascended to the throne of Israel, and Zadok was numbered among his select leaders. However, after many years of rule, David's son Absalom suddenly sought to overthrow his government. [64]Absalom draws the favour of the people and he secures the services of the great counsellor, Ahithophel the Gilonite, who was leader of David's counsellors. So after many years of establishing the Davidic government and rule, this high priest Zadok is called upon to make a choice. He could have complained that he was not able to move on with David, because he had established a name for himself as a "seer or Prophet"[65] in Israel.

He could have made several excuses as to why he should stay, but instead he flees with David into the wilderness, because he knew in his heart that God was with

---

[63] Hebrews 13: 12-13
[64] 2 Samuel 15:13
[65] 2 Samuel 15:27

David. He knew that the anointing of God rested heavily upon David, so he followed David, bearing the "Ark of the Covenant"[66].

But that is not all. David then calls upon Zadok and his sons to go back into the camp and act as spies[67]. He reminds Zadok that he was a seer and that he should take the "Ark of the Covenant" back into city and sense the timing and mind of the Lord about his (David's) return to rule. We then go on to read an awesome account of a spy thriller (the likes of a "*James Bond*" movie):

"Then Hushai said to Zadok and Abiathar the priests, "Thus and so Ahithophel advised Absalom and the elders of Israel, and thus and so I have advised. Now therefore, send quickly and tell David, saying, 'Do not spend this night in the plains of the wilderness, but speedily cross over, lest the king and all the people who are with him be swallowed up.' "Now Jonathan and Ahimaaz stayed at En Rogel, for they dared not be seen coming into the city; so a female servant would come and tell them, and they would go and tell King David. Nevertheless a lad saw them and told Absalom. But both of them went away quickly and came to a man's house in Bahurim, who had a well in his court; and they went down into it. Then the woman took and spread a covering over the well's mouth, and spread ground grain on it; and the thing was not known. And when Absalom's servants came to the woman at the house, they said, "Where are Ahimaaz and Jonathan?" So the

---

[66] 2 Samuel 15: 24-29
[67] 2 Samuel 15:25-27

woman said to them, "They have gone over the water brook." And when they had searched and could not find them, they returned to Jerusalem. Now it came to pass, after they had departed, that they came up out of the well and went and told King David, and said to David, "Arise and cross over the water quickly. For thus has Ahithophel advised against you." 2 Samuel 17: 15-21

This whole sequence of events takes place because of the statement that David made to Zadok:

"Then the king said to Zadok, 'Carry the ark of God back into the city. If I find favour in the eyes of the Lord, He will bring me back and show me both it and His dwelling place. 'But if He says thus: 'I have no delight in you,' here I am, let Him do to me as seems good to Him.'" 2 Samuel 15:25-26

Saints, this is the very same attitude that we must possess in the current move of God. If this apostolic/prophetic restoration is of God, He will grant us the favour, grace, resource, personnel, and breakthrough, everything we need to ensure that His Glory is seen in all the nations of the earth. If not, then the sooner that this entire thing dies the better, but we know that it is of the Lord, *Hallelujah!*

Regardless of the opposition, the whisperings of the devil, the religious system of man, God's Glory will be seen in *all* the earth!

After all is said and done with Absalom, we read that

[68]he dies a horrible death and God restores the kingdom back to David. David restores true government back to the people of Israel and just when one thought it was all over for Zadok, and he could now rest and enjoy peace, up rises Adonijah. [69]He confers with Joab and Abiathar, the high priest, - who was Zadok's long-standing friend and fellow high priest - to wrest the throne from David. Through this, Abiathar betrayed David's trust; however, [70]Zadok remained true to the move of God and stuck by David's side.

A lesson can be learned from the actions of Abiathar, he almost made it faithfully through the reign of David, but just when it mattered the most, he betrayed both David and Zadok. We must be willing to go with the move of God to the very end; we must be apostolic people and be able to finish.

As we trace the descendants of Zadok, we see [71]Jothan reigning in Judah and doing what was right in the sight of the Lord. [72]Azariah, who functioned under Hezekiah in the days of reform in Israel, was another descendant of Zadok. [73]Ezra, the priest who returned from Babylonian captivity to rebuild the temple of the Lord, was also a descendant of Zadok. And of course the sons of Zadok were very present in Ezekiel's vision of the end-time temple.

---

[68] 2 Samuel 18: 9-10
[69] 1 Kings 1:5-27
[70] 1 Kings 1:8,26,39
[71] 2 Kings 15: 32-37
[72] 2 Chronicles 31:10
[73] Ezra 7: 1- 6

These sons of Zadok are represented today by those who will press through every obstacle; those who embrace the true apostolic/prophetic anointing; those who are willing to give up everything including fame and fortune to embrace the move of God. These are the ones who will minister both before the Lord and to the people - the true difference between the Holy and the profane.

It is with a great stirring in my spirit that I write this book to encourage all of us to step into, and flow in, the anointing of this great high priest of the Lord. I call it *"The Zadok Anointing"*. As a matter of fact, that is what the Lord spoke to me in a vision one Sunday night about Zadok. It was so real that when I awoke the message was still very clear to me. Let us keep our eyes focused on that which the Lord is declaring in this hour. Do not be sidetracked by the distractions of the devil, but keep pressing just like the Apostle Paul did when he declared:

"Not that I have already attained, or am already perfected; but I press on, that I may lay hold of that for which Christ Jesus has also laid hold of me. but one thing I do, forgetting those things which are behind and reaching forward to those things which are ahead, I press toward the goal for the prize of the upward call of God in Christ Jesus." Philippians 3:12-14

"But the priests, the Levites, the sons of Zadok, who kept charge of My sanctuary when the children of Israel went astray from Me, they shall come near Me to minister to Me; and they shall stand before Me to offer to Me the fat and the blood," says the Lord GOD. They

shall enter My sanctuary, and they shall come near My table to minister to Me, and they shall keep My charge. And it shall be, whenever they enter the gates of the *inner court, that they shall put on linen garments; no wool* shall come upon them while they minister within the gates of the inner court or within the house. They shall have linen turbans on their heads and linen trousers on their bodies; *they shall not clothe themselves with anything that causes sweat.* When they go out to the outer court, *to the outer court to the people, they shall take off their garments in which they have ministered,* leave them in the holy chambers, and put on other garments; and in their holy garments they shall not sanctify the people. They shall neither shave their heads nor let their hair grow long; but *they shall keep their hair well trimmed. No priest shall drink wine when he enters the inner court.* They *shall not take as wife a widow or a divorced woman,* but take virgins of the descendants of the house of Israel, or widows of priests. And *they shall teach My people the difference between the holy and the unholy,* and cause them to discern *between the unclean and the clean. In controversy they shall stand as judges, and judge it according to My judgments.* They shall keep My laws and My statutes in all My appointed meetings, and they shall hallow My Sabbaths." Ezekiel 44:15-24 (Italics added)

There are several very powerful principles we can draw from the preceding verses about the requirements of the *Zadok Anointing.*

- **They shall come near Me, to minister unto Me (verse 15):** This is an awesome command and tremendous privilege, but we must note that this came about because of the heart position of Zadok and his sons. They kept the move of God alive when all the other leaders went astray. Keeping the *"move of God"* alive is not accomplished by being people pleasers; or by participating in *"spiritual politics"*, but by maintaining a place for God's presence to dwell.

- **The garment that was worn to minister before the Lord was linen (verses 17-18):** Linen is symbolic of [74]purity and righteousness. It also reminds us of our Lord and Saviour, Jesus Christ as they wrapped Him for burial. [75]He was wrapped in fine linen symbolizing the righteousness of what He did by His death. This shows that any ministering that is to be done before the Lord must be on the basis of the finished work of Calvary. Part of the *"Zadok Anointing"* is the dynamic of the death of Jesus working in us. There must be a complete separation from the *"self life"*.

- **They were not to wear anything that produced sweat (verse 18):** This speaks of a death to human effort. Human effort produces sin (represented by sweat). Remember Joshua, the high priest, in Zechariah 3:1-5. We must be able to function as *"Sons of Zadok"* from a position of rest. (Remember Adam was created on the sixth day, so his first day was God's

---

[74] Revelation 15:6; 19:8,14
[75] Mark 15:45-46

day of rest. It was from this realm that the first Adam began to function.) Likewise with Jesus, He entered into the rest of the Father and from that position He functioned. The Apostle Paul dealt with that situation as [76]he spoke to the dwellers of Mars Hill. God does not dwell in temples made with men's hands nor is He worshipped with men's hands as though He needed anything. As we, the true *"Sons of Zadok"*, come before the Lord; let us not bring any sweat before Him. Function from our position of rest.

- **They were not to minister before the people in their linen garments (verse 19):** This is very significant, because the reason for them going to the people in the first place was to bring divine discernment between that which was holy and that, which was not. So in essence, God knew that among the mass multitude of the people sin existed and the priests were not to defile their garments. These garments were to be preserved unto the Lord. There is a dimension of our lives as priests, which must be exclusively the Lord's.

- **They were to maintain well-trimmed hair (verse 20):** This represents a seemingly *"normal"* lifestyle. They were not to appear to humanity as being separate by anything external. As with the garments, our hairstyle must not set us apart. Remember Jesus often times warned not to let our righteousness be an outward show. As a matter of fact, He declared that when we

---

[76] Acts 17:22-25

[77]fast we must not even appear to men as though we were. So the Lord wants us to lead normal lifestyles in the midst of a great and powerful ministry unto and for Him.

- **They were not to drink wine when they entered the inner court (verse 21)** - Entering the inner court represents a deliberate time of meeting with God. Wine here represents a false anointing. It speaks about a man made control over our life. The Bible declares:

  "See then that you walk circumspectly, not as fools but as wise, redeeming the time, because the days are evil. Therefore do not be unwise, but understand what the will of the Lord is. And do not be drunk with wine, in which is dissipation; but be filled with the Spirit." Ephesians 5:15-18

The Holy Spirit must be in control of our lives as we come into the presence of Almighty God. It is the Holy Spirit that will aid in our times of intercession. It is He who will bring the divine revelation to go back to minister to the people. Let us constantly be, in a state of *"being"* filled, with the Holy Spirit.

- **The sons of Zadok were to be very careful whom they married (verse 22):** This speaks to us of the careful choice we are to make when networking. Marriage speaks of an intimate joining. There are some ministries God will want us to minister to but not have

---

[77] Matthew 6:16-18

an intimate relationship with. This is very significant, as the Prophet declares in Amos 3:3, *"Can two walk together, unless they are agreed?"* There are some churches and ministries today who are widowed (no sense of relationship or accountability) or divorced (wilful breaking of covenant relationship); to these types we are not to join ourselves. However, we can enter into relationship with types of ministries that are widowed because of the death of a priest (true anointed legitimate government of God). Likewise, we must be careful whom we link and join ourselves to. In the book of Isaiah, the Lord reveals to the Prophet the things that are to come. He shows him, the eventual state of the endtime church in chapter two, and then goes on to reveal to him the tremendous cleansing that will take place. In the context of this we read the following:

> "And in that day seven women shall take hold of one man, saying, 'We will eat our own food and wear our own apparel; Only let us be called by your name, to take away our reproach.'" Isaiah 4:1

We are now entering into these days, as apostles and prophets are being restored. God is now moving in the realm of *"networks."* However, we have to be careful in *"networking"*, as some will establish networks with the intention of seeing how many churches they can have operating "under" them. In some cases these *"networks"* will be built with *"seven women"* (representing local churches) taking hold of one man (representing an "apostolic/prophetic network"), but without any true representation of the "network." They will only assume the name but not the inner identity and vision of the "network." Many of these kinds of "networks" will crumble as we press further into the true dimension of what God is doing in this hour. Networks that are built on *strong relationship and sincerity* will survive, as the purification of the Spirit of God begins in this hour. These will flow and function in the spirit of *"The sons of Zadok"*.

- **A greater sense of discernment was upon the sons of Zadok (verse 23):** They were able to teach the people the difference between the holy and the profane, between the clean and the unclean. As we minister before the Lord, we will know this dimension of discernment, as we will need it for survival in these last days.

- **Controversy surrounded them as they brought the judgements of the Lord (verse 24):** We are to be prepared for controversy, as this is part of the dynamics of kingdom life. It also comes with the apostolic/prophetic anointing. This anointing thrives in difficult situations. However the factor that will ensure that we bring proper judgements in the face of opposition is the quality time we spend in the presence of Almighty God.

These represent some of the dynamics of the *"Zadok Anointing"* into which we are called to walk and function, if we are to have the breakthrough and success the Lord has intended for us. Let us be focused as we continue to proclaim a mighty Jesus in every territory and in the nations of the earth. Expect the Lord to come and interact with us, give us greater dimensions of discernment and release to us the technology for accurate advance of His Kingdom through His apostles and prophets here and now:

"Then He brought me back to the outer gate of the sanctuary which faces toward the east, *but it was shut. And the LORD said to me, "This gate shall be shut; it shall not be opened, and no man shall enter by it, because the LORD God of Israel has entered by it; therefore it shall be shut.* As for the prince, because he is the prince, he may sit in it to eat bread before the LORD; he shall enter by way of the vestibule of the gateway, and go out the same way." Ezekiel 44:1-3 (Italics added)

As we continue, I want to bring to our attention the issue of the Shut Gate. In this scripture the Lord was revealing to the Prophet and priest Ezekiel the dynamics of the end-time Church. From *chapters 40-43* he gets a clear understanding and blueprint of the temple and all its furnishings. However, in Ezekiel 44, the Lord begins to show him those who will be admitted to the temple and the requirements of the priesthood. As he begins this leg of the journey, the very first thing the Lord shows him is the closed gate:

"And the LORD said to me, "This gate shall be shut; it shall not be opened, and no man shall enter by it, because the LORD God of Israel has entered by it; therefore it shall be shut." Ezekiel 44:2

This gate was God's entry point and it was securely

shut. No one else was to pass through this gate. We must have this "shut gate" in our ministries, in our churches, in our businesses and in our personal lives. This is the area of our life that must be reserved for the Holy Spirit. This represents the entry point of the Lord into our ministries, and I say to you that no one, and I mean no one, is to tamper with His entry! Likewise, in our prayer the Lord must have free course, He must be able to enter and shut the door without any questions being asked, and He reserves that right.

There is also another dynamic here that we need to look at. The scripture says that the gate was shut because "the Lord God of Israel has entered by it", signifying a sense of permanence to the Lord's stay. As a matter of fact, this is supported by the fact that the very last thing Ezekiel saw was the gate of the city and its name:

> "These are the exits of the city. On the north side, measuring four thousand five hundred cubits (the gates of the city shall be named after the tribes of Israel)... All the way around shall be eighteen thousand cubits; and the name of the city from that day shall be: *THE LORD IS THERE.*"   Ezekiel 48:30-31, 35 (Italics added)

This tells us that once the Lord arrived He had every intention of staying. We must be confident of the fact that we are building according to the blueprint the Lord has for our ministry. We are preparing the way for the Lord's entry into our places of worship, and when He arrives it will be with a sense of *Permanence*! Again let me re-emphasize - once we build it according to His specifications and standard, He *will* come and live in our midst, and His banner *"THE LORD IS HERE"* will be sealed upon us, and our ministries:

However, there is another significant dynamic that takes place at "the shut gate".   "As for the *prince*, because he is the *prince*, he may sit in it to eat bread before the Lord; he shall enter by way of the vestibule of the gateway, and go out the same way." Ezekiel 44:3 (Italics added)

This is an awesome verse of scripture in the context of the events that were to take place at this gate.

But who is this *prince*, and why is he to be given such privileges? I submit to you that this prince refers to Jacob. Let us go back to Jacob's life and see what caused him to be a prince and what could have caused him to be given these privileges:

"And he arose that night and took his two wives, his two female servants, and his eleven sons, and crossed over the ford of Jabbok. He took them, sent them over the brook, and sent over what he had. Then Jacob was left alone; and a Man wrestled with him until the breaking of day. Now when He saw that He did not prevail against him, He touched the socket of his hip; and the socket of Jacob's hip was out of joint as He wrestled with him. And He said, "Let Me go, for the day breaks." But he said, "I will not let You go unless You bless me!" So He said to him, "What is your

name?" And he said, "Jacob."   And He said, "Your
name shall no longer be called Jacob, but Israel; for you
have struggled with God and with men, and have
prevailed."   Then Jacob asked, saying, "Tell me Your
name, I pray."   And He said, "Why is it that you ask
about My name?" And He blessed him there.   And
Jacob called the name of the place Peniel: "For I have
seen God face to face, and my life is preserved."
Genesis 32:22-30

Here we read that Jacob wrestled with the Lord.   This is
truly awesome, and the reason for that wrestling match is
very significant.   Jacob's name in Hebrew is Supplanter,
which means - "to take the place of another, especially by
trickery".

Jacob represents the believer who is called of God but
not yet in the place where God can use him/her to his/her
full potential and call.   Jacob also represents the believer
who doesn't have a *"Shut Gate"* in his or her life.

**However, on that particular night, Jacob came to a
place of a "divine encounter" and he owned up to his
true identity.**   The account in Genesis 32:22-30 was to
deal with the whole issue of Jacob's nature.   *When the
Lord confronted him and asked what is your name.   He
was really asking what is your nature?   Really, who are
you?*   In order to have a *"Shut Gate"* in our lives we must
answer that question - *"Who are you?"* When you are faced
with the Lord by yourself, deep down on the inside, who
are you?

most important.

Jacob's reply triggered a divine response that changed the course of the history of his life and he entered into his true call. He declared to the Lord, "my name is Jacob". Yes Lord, I am a "Supplanter", I will not try to hide my true nature from you. I am ready to face up to reality; I am ready to deal with all the issues of my life.

It was at that time the Lord entered into Jacob's life and "shut the gate", as Jacob declared in verse 30 "*For I have seen God face to face, and my life is preserved.*" Yes, God called Jacob even from his mother's womb, but it was not until this time that the Lord really entered into his life in a truly permanent way.

From that encounter the Lord changed his name to Israel, (In Hebrew Yisrael meaning - "*as a prince you have power with God*") and his prophetic destiny was released. The "*Shut Gate*" in his life was known by the dislocating of his hip socket. From that encounter, Israel, formerly Jacob walked with a limp[78].

We know that once we are saved, the Lord comes into our lives, and that is very true. However, we also know that there is an arrival that the Lord wants to make in us as we mature in Him. Remember the early saints in the book of Acts; they were all followers of Jesus, but He told them to tarry and wait for His arrival, via the Holy Spirit. They could have argued that they knew Him, and that they walked with Him for many years and that they were ready to step out and demonstrate Him to the world. However,

---

[78] Genesis 32:31-32

they chose to obey Him and the rest is history. There was an incredible arrival of the Lord on the day of [79]Pentecost, and the Lord shut the gate and moved powerfully with them.

Another interesting example is found in the book of Malachi. Here we see the people of God seeking after Him. They are not heathens; they are the people of God. This was not a casual seeking, it was very deliberate and determined, and so the Lord responds with one of His "arrivals":

"And *the Lord whom you seek, will suddenly come to His temple*, even the messenger of the covenant, in whom you delight. Behold, He is coming" says the Lord of Hosts. "But who can endure the day of His coming? And who can stand when He appears? For *He is like a refiner's fire* And like launderer's soap. *He will sit as a refiner* and a purifier of silver; *He will purify the sons of Levi, And purge them as gold and silver, That they may offer to the LORD An offering in righteousness.* "Then the offering of Judah and Jerusalem Will be pleasant to the LORD, As in the days of old, As in former years. And *I will come near you for judgment; I will be a swift witness Against* sorcerers, Against adulterers, Against perjurers, *Against those who exploit wage earners and widows and orphans*, And against those who turn away an alien--Because they do not fear Me," Says the LORD of hosts.'"   Malachi 3:1-5 (Italics added)

---

[79] Acts 2:1-4

The end result of this arrival, just like in Ezekiel's temple, is that the priests were purified and a mighty move of God took place.

As we continue, we must understand that the Lord does not only give us the status of "*The Sons of Zadok*" – (*a type of the priesthood of the believer*) but also of "*The Prince*" – (*a type of the royalty of the believer*). He wants to make His permanent entry into our midst and reveal His full destiny for us. The Lord is about to make an arrival to take His end-time Church to her full destiny. God wants our apostolic decrees and our prophetic declarations to become a "Shut Gate" for Him! He wants our ministries to have a "Shut Gate". He wants our lives to have a "*Shut Gate*". There is such a sense of *God* in this hour as He restores His apostles and prophets. May He have His full way in all that we do that He may get maximum *Glory*!

Chapter Six – Part II
Qualifications And Blemishes Of The Priesthood II

As was said before, when the Lord was instituting the Aaronic priesthood, He established certain criteria for its smooth and proper functioning. The following portion gives the general, foundational outline for the priesthood, which we will be exploring:

"And the LORD spoke to Moses, saying, "Speak to Aaron, saying: 'No man of your descendants in succeeding generations, who has any defect, may approach to offer the bread of his God. For *any man who has a defect shall not approach*: a man *blind or lame*, who has a *marred face* or any *limb too long*, a man who has a *broken foot or broken hand*, or is a *hunchback or a dwarf*, or a man who has a *defect in his eye, or eczema or scab*, or is a *eunuch*. No man of the descendants of Aaron the priest, who has a defect, shall come near to offer the offerings made by fire to the LO-

RD. He has a defect; he shall not come near to offer the bread of his God. *He may eat the bread of his God, both the most holy and the holy; only he shall not go near the veil or approach the altar, because he has a defect, lest he profane My sanctuaries; for I the LORD sanctify them.*'" Leviticus 21:16-23 (Italics added)

As we read in the preceding text, even though one was born into the tribe of Levi, there was still a selection process for divine function. He was not disqualified from being a member of the tribe, or from partaking of the *bread of God*; he was only barred from divine functions.

This has relevance to us today, as it is similar to the *Royal Priesthood* of God. If one has a defect, that does not disqualify him from being a member of the Church, but disqualifies him from functioning in his leadership capacity, until the defect is corrected, Leviticus 21: 21-23 clearly states this:

> "No man of the descendants of Aaron the priest, who has a defect, shall come near to offer the offerings made by fire to the LORD. He has a defect; he shall not come near to offer the bread of his God. *He may eat the bread of his God, both the most holy and the holy; only he shall not go near the veil or approach the altar, because he has a defect, lest he profane My sanctuaries; for I the LORD sanctify them.*'" (Italics added)

However, we know that in many Christian circles this is not happening. There are many who have defects and are ministering the *bread of God* to the people. The bread of God represents the revelation of Christ – the Word of God! The Word of God clearly states that he could eat, but not minister.

We need to understand that we are in a battle, and the intensity of the battle is not primarily for geographical territory as it is for our souls. This is the prime target of the anti-Christ; he wants to sit in the temple[80] – (the true temple which is [81]our body and the Church[82]). This is why there is going to be a strong emphasis on purity in these last days.

We saw this principle operate when Jesus was about to be crucified and Peter rose up in absolute denial of his knowledge of Jesus:

> "And the Lord said, "Simon, Simon! Indeed, Satan has asked for you, that he may sift you as wheat. But I have prayed for you, that your faith should not fail; *and when you have returned to Me, strengthen your brethren*." But he said to Him, "Lord, I am ready to go with You, both to prison and to death." Then He said, "I tell you, Peter, the rooster shall not crow this day before you will deny three times that you know Me.""
> Luke 22:31-34 (Italics added)

We know that this came to pass and Peter fell away, however, the Lord ensured that he was fully restored

---

[80] 2 Thessalonians 2:4
[81] 1 Corinthians 6:19
[82] Ephesians 2: 19-22

before stepping back into the place of divine function of dealing *"the bread of God"* to the people. A renewed and energized [83]Peter was the first Apostle to minister to the multitude on the Day of Pentecost, after the Holy Spirit had fallen.

This is why there is such an intense cry from the hearts of men and women of God all over the earth, declaring *"Purify Your people O God, cleanse us with Your fire O God!"* Houses of prayer are being established as people press into God. The breed of leadership that is emerging in the Church will be consumed with Holiness of the Lord and they will cause a dividing line to come, in the professing ranks of Christianity. There is a people rising in the earth who will fulfill the word of the Lord in the book of Revelations which says:

"And he said to me, *"Do not seal the words of the prophecy of this book, for the time is at hand.* He who is unjust, let him be unjust still; he who is filthy, let him be filthy still; he who is righteous, let him be righteous still; he who is holy, let him be holy still. And behold, *I am coming quickly, and My reward is with Me, to give to every one according to his work.* I am the Alpha and the Omega, the Beginning and the End, the First and the Last." *Blessed are those who do His commandments*, that they may have the right to the tree of life, and may enter through the gates into the city. But outside are dogs and sorcerers and sexually

---

[83] Acts 2:14

immoral and murderers and idolaters, and whoever loves and practices a lie. *I, Jesus, have sent My angel to testify to you these things in the churches.* I am the Root and the Offspring of David, the Bright and Morning Star." *And the Spirit and the bride say, "Come" And let him who hears say, "Come"* And let him who thirsts come Whoever desires, let him take the water of life freely."   Revelation 22:10-17 (Italics added)

So this is the time more than ever for us to make it right with God, this is the time to step into covenants of obedience with the Lord and establish it in your heart to walk pure before the Lord. This is the time to receive the grace of God and not frustrate it. This is the time to say, *Lord, search my heart and see if there is any wicked way in me and cleanse me so that I could walk pure before You."*

Oh there is such a cry in my heart as I write, as I know that there is arising a people who will not compromise the word of God. Some are rising from the ashes of a past life of hurt, pain and disillusionment; some are coming home as the prodigal; some have been crying out to the Lord like the son who never went astray, waiting for his inheritance; still some are young, now born again, fresh, new believers; some are leaders of churches, ministries, networks – wherever they are, there is one cry and one cry only – *"More of You Lord, more of You!"*

In the light of this let us look at some of the defects that can disqualify us from functioning in one's full *"Royal Priesthood"* capacity.

We are speaking here about the ability to minister the life of God to others. Remember, ministry is much more than the ability to articulate a given language; it is the ability to impart Spirit and Life into people. Jesus said it this way – *"It is the Spirit who gives life; the flesh profits nothing. The words that I speak to you are spirit, and they are life."* John 6:63

He also said – *"...I have come that they may have life, and that they may have it more abundantly."* John 10:10 The Apostle Paul expressed it this way – *"For I long to see you, that I may impart to you some spiritual gift, so that you may be established."'"* Romans 1:11

Please understand that ministering from a wrong spirit or lifestyle can potentially damage others and certainly [84]disqualify us - Impurities must be dealt with.

Leviticus 21: 16 - 23
These physical defects represent spiritual areas that must be restructured in the New Testament priest.

Blindness
This is the inability to see. Spiritually this speaks of a lack of, or defective spiritual vision. If a person or ministry does not have a definable vision from God they should not be leading God's people. Proverbs 29: 18 declare: *"Where there is no vision, the people perish..."* *KJV*

The word vision is the Hebrew word *"Chazon"* - which

---

[84] Matthew 7:21-23

is rendered; a prophetic vision, dream, oracle, revelation; especially the kind of revelation that comes through sight, namely a vision from God. This word also carries the expression of what is termed "prophetic revelation" or the revelation that was received by the prophets.

For example:
"The vision of Isaiah the son of Amoz, which he saw concerning Judah and Jerusalem in the days of Uzziah, Jotham, Ahaz, and Hezekiah, kings of Judah." Isaiah 1:1

"Son of man, look, the house of Israel is saying, 'The vision that he sees is for many days from now, and he prophesies of times far off.'" Ezekiel 12:27 "In the third year of the reign of King Belshazzar a vision appeared to me--to me, Daniel--after the one that appeared to me the first time. I saw in the vision, and it so happened while I was looking, that I was in Shushan, the citadel, which is in the province of Elam; and I saw in the vision that I was by the River Ulai." Daniel 8:1-2

We need to understand that *vision* holds the key to proper functioning of leadership.

The prophets understood God's counsel and as a *"prophetic people"* we will also flow in the same understanding. Proverbs 29:18 shows that when a society lacks *"prophetic revelation"* from God, such a people head in the direction of anarchy:

"Where there is no revelation, the people cast off restraint; But happy is he who keeps the law."

"Where there is no vision, the people perish: but he that keepeth the law, happy is he." *KJV*

This is the reason leadership must be able to have vision.

Importance of Vision - It must be communicated:

"I will stand my watch And set myself on the rampart, And watch to see what He will say to me, And what I will answer when I am corrected. Then the LORD answered me and said: *"Write the vision And make it plain* on tablets, That *he may run who reads* it." Habakkuk 2:1-2 (Italics added)

There is a movement from conception to action. – The progression is – *see/perceive => write => clarify => communicate => produce action.*

The ability to function accurately, with accountability and full authority, depends upon our understanding of the vision[85].

Psalms 133 gives us the technology of the spiritual flow of vision. Whatever is on the head will flow down into the body that is united in vision and purpose:

---

[85] Hosea 4:6

"Behold, how good and how pleasant it is For brethren to dwell together in unity! It is like the precious oil upon the head, Running down on the beard, The beard of Aaron, Running down on the edge of his garments. It is like the dew of Hermon, Descending upon the mountains of Zion; For there the LORD commanded the blessing--Life forevermore."

Here is a powerful example of the importance of vision and what happens when it is communicated and received properly.

Moses' Example: Numbers 11:16, 24-30
"And the LORD said unto Moses, Gather unto me seventy men of the elders of Israel, whom thou knowest to be the elders of the people, and officers over them; and bring them unto the tabernacle of the congregation, that they may stand there with thee... So Moses went out and told the people the words of the LORD, and he gathered the *seventy men of the elders* of the people and placed them around the tabernacle. *Then the LORD came down in the cloud, and spoke to him, and took of the Spirit that was upon him, and placed the same upon the seventy elders*; and it happened, when the Spirit rested upon them, that they prophesied, although they never did so again. *But two men had remained in the camp*: the name of one was Eldad, and the name of the other Medad. *And the Spirit rested upon them. Now they were among those listed, but who had not gone out to the tabernacle; yet they prophesied in the camp.* And a young man ran and told Moses, and said, "Eldad and Medad are prophesying in the camp." So Joshua

the son of Nun, Moses' assistant, one of his choice men, answered and said, "Moses my lord, forbid them!" Then Moses said to him, "Are you zealous for my sake? Oh that all the LORD's people were prophets and that the LORD would put His Spirit upon them!" And Moses returned to the camp, both he and the elders of Israel." (Italics added)

What an awesome event! Even though Eldad and Medad were not physically in the same geographical location as Moses and the others, they received of the same Spirit because they were one with the vision and leadership of Moses.

Hence the reason that *blindness* brings disqualification.

Lameness

Indicates the man who can see and discern what God is doing but does not have the ability to walk in it. Can preach but cannot operate in the preached truth. He is qualified to be a Pharisee:

"Then Jesus spoke to the multitudes and to His disciples, saying: "The scribes and the Pharisees sit in Moses' seat. Therefore whatever they tell you to observe, that observe and do, but do not do according to their works; for they say, and do not do. For they bind heavy burdens, hard to bear, and lay them on men's shoulders; but they themselves will not move them with one of their fingers." Matthew 23:1-4

The Apostle James declared this:

"But be doers of the word, and not hearers only, deceiving yourselves. For if anyone is a hearer of the word and not a doer, he is like a man observing his natural face in a mirror; for he observes himself, goes away, and immediately forgets what kind of man he was. But he who looks into the perfect law of liberty and continues in it, and is not a forgetful hearer but a doer of the work, this one will be blessed in what he does." James 1:22-25

In the book of Acts we have a wonderful picture of this condition and the subsequent breakthrough for the person involved. In Acts 3 we have the situation of a man who was lame from his mother's womb and was laid at the gate of the temple, which was called Beautiful. This man could represent the man of God who has sight, but is unable to walk in what he sees. He is at the right place but cannot walk out what is being ministered. Here is the text:

"Now Peter and John went up together to the temple at the hour of prayer, the ninth hour. And a certain man lame from his mother's womb was carried, whom they laid daily at the gate of the temple which is called Beautiful, to ask alms from those who entered the temple; *who, seeing Peter and John* about to go into the temple, asked for alms. And fixing his eyes on him, with John, Peter said, "*Look at us.*" So he gave them his attention, expecting to receive something from them. Then Peter said, "Silver and gold I do not have, but what I do have I give you: *In the name of Jesus Christ of Nazareth, rise up and walk.*" And he took him by the right hand and lifted him up, and

immediately his feet and ankle bones received strength.
So he, leaping up, *stood and walked* and entered the
temple with them-- walking, leaping, and praising God.
And all the people *saw him walking* and praising God.
Then they knew that it was he who sat begging alms at
the Beautiful Gate of the temple; and they were filled
with wonder and amazement at what had happened to
him." Acts 3 1 – 10 (Italics added)

This man represents the many today who live off the
temple; they have all the right words being preached to
them, they are by the temple everyday. Their lives are
filled with silver and gold and they do not realize their dire
need for true apostolic ministry. However, this man came
to the place of taking a closer look at true apostolic
ministry that was passing by. He thought surely I could
receive a good word or "*a touch*" from these men. And
sure enough he did. His lame condition was completely
healed. I say to you today, if you find yourself in the
position of not being able to walk out what you are seeing,
this is the time to find some apostolic ministry that can
deliver you.

Peter made one of the most precious statements that
epitomize the heart cry of true God-Ordained leadership –
"Look at us".

This is one of the most powerful statements that can
come from God ordained leadership. What a firm yet
tender statement! This is truly a sign of apostolic
leadership, leading by example.

The type of leaders that the Lord is bringing forth in these last days is what is called *"servant-leaders"* who will lead by example. They will surely walk in the spirit and power of Elijah and would turn the hearts of people towards the Lord by their demonstrative lifestyle:

> *"Then Elijah said* to all the people, "*Come near to me.*" So all the people came near to him. And he repaired the altar of the LORD that was broken down." 1 Kings 18:30 (Italics added)

They would be like the apostle Paul as he declared to the saints in Corinth and Philippi:

> "For though you might have ten thousand instructors in Christ, yet you do not have many fathers; for in Christ Jesus I have begotten you through the gospel. Therefore *I urge you, imitate me.* For this reason I have sent Timothy to you, who is my beloved and faithful son in the Lord, *who will remind you of my ways in Christ*, as I teach everywhere in every church." 1 Corinthians 4:15-17 (Italics added)

> *"Imitate me*, just as *I also imitate Christ."* 1 Corinthians 11:1 (Italics added)

> "Brethren, *join in following my example*, and note those who so walk, *as you have us for a pattern."* Philippians 3:17 (Italics added)

Jesus – of course He was and still is, the greatest leader of all times and He has led by example even to the death on the cross[86].   You must be able to walk the talk if you are to be an effective *royal-priest* in these last days.

Flat Nose

Our nose represents our smellers. Among other uses, it is used to ascertain if something is pure or rotten before it is eaten.   Its position speaks of its importance.   This describes our ability to discern.

This is an extremely important skill for leaders in this hour. We are living in the days of increasing deception. As the Lord restores apostles back to His Church, we are mandated to [87]try them who say they are apostles and are not; however this will call for heightened discernment.

The person with a *"spiritually flat nose"* is disqualified to minister the life of God to others. The Word of God declares in Hebrew:

"For though by this time you ought to be teachers, you need someone to teach you again the first principles of the oracles of God; and you have come to need milk and not solid food. For everyone who partakes only of milk is unskilled in the word of righteousness, for he is a babe. But solid food belongs to those who are of full age, that is, those who by reason of use have their senses exercised to discern both good and evil." Hebrews 5:12-14

[86] Hebrews 12:1-4
[87] Revelation 2:2

A lack of discernment qualifies one to remain a babe in Christ and in need of milk. If your nose is flat you need to be taught rather than find yourself teaching. We are in a war for territory; the kingdoms of this world must become the kingdoms of our Lord and of His Christ. God is looking for warhorses to ride into the battle in these last days. He wants us to be like the horse described in the book of Job:

"Have you given the horse strength? Have you clothed his neck with thunder? Can you frighten him like a locust? His majestic snorting strikes terror. He paws in the valley, and rejoices in his strength; He gallops into the clash of arms. He mocks at fear, and is not frightened; Nor does he turn back from the sword. The quiver rattles against him, The glittering spear and javelin. He devours the distance with fierceness and rage; Nor does he come to a halt because the trumpet has sounded. At the blast of the trumpet he says, 'Aha!' He *smells* the battle from afar, The thunder of captains and shouting." Job 39: 19-25 (Italics added)

In the Hebrew language there are about five different words that translate discern. However, the one that is used in Malachi 3:18 – *"Then you shall again discern Between the righteous and the wicked, Between one who serves God And one who does not serve Him."*- is the word *"raha"* and it carries the sense of one knowing after careful scrutiny and experience. It is what happens when the Lord suddenly comes to His temple and purifies the priests; there is a return to justice and the way of the Lord. A separation takes place and those that fear the Lord come into this place of keen discernment.

Apostolic Purity is the key to having keen discernment return to the House of God.

There are also several Greek words that translate discern. However, the one that is used in the following text is the word *"diakrino"*, and it means - expressing close and distinct acquaintance with, or a critical knowledge of things. Thoroughly separate, to withdraw from, or by implication oppose. If one's nose is flat, discernment is difficult, if not impossible and there will be no way to ascertain what is being served to the people of God. The husbandman must be first partaker of the fruit.

"But solid food belongs to those who are of full age, that is, those who by reason of use have their senses exercised to *discern* both good and evil." Hebrews 5:14

Deformed or Superfluous

A condition of imbalance: e.g. if one foot is shorter than the other or having six toes instead of five or some extra, unnecessary growth. The Living Bible states it this way:

"For instance, if a man is blind or lame, or has a broken nose or *any extra fingers or toes*." Lev: 21:18 (Italics added)

This indicates ministry that is *"one-sided"* or *unbalanced.* We must release the whole counsel of God as the Apostle Paul did:

"For I have not shunned to declare to you the whole counsel of God." Acts 20:27

This holds true for even some *"apostolic and prophetic camps,"* as there is a serious imbalance in the diet given to the saints.

In many ways the spiritual body is similar to the natural body. If we were to only feed the natural body on milk, from infancy to adulthood, serious health problems would occur. As a matter of fact we can experience health problems if we eat an imbalanced diet. In like manner, we can become unhealthy spiritually if we do not have a balanced diet of the things of God.

Broken Foot

This is different from being lame; this is an injury that is not restored. The foot in the New Testament represents our walk in Christ. In the book of Ephesians in describing the believer's armour, the feet are shod with the gospel:

"Therefore take up the whole armour of God, that you may be able to withstand in the evil day, and having done all, to stand. Stand therefore, having girded your waist with truth, having put on the breastplate of righteousness, and having *shod your feet with the preparation of the gospel of peace..."* Ephesians 6:13-16 (Italics added)

If your foot is broken, your ability to walk out the gospel will be severely hindered. A broken foot reveals one being damaged in their walk with God and never being fully restored. He is "*spiritually disabled.*" He is not able to keep pace with others; therefore he walks alone.

There is no relationship and support from other ministries and no plurality in his government system.

No sharing of his pulpit and he cannot walk straight. The body of Christ is not discerned and you are unsure of his standing:

> "Brethren, join in following my example, and note those who so walk, as you have us for a pattern. For many walk, of whom I have told you often, and now tell you even weeping, that they are the enemies of the cross of Christ: whose end is destruction, whose god is their belly, and whose glory is in their shame--who set their mind on earthly things." Philippians 3:17-19

The Word of God strictly warns that such people are unfaithful. One is never sure about them. A ministry or minister that has a broken foot cannot be relied upon:

> "Confidence in an *unfaithful man* in time of trouble Is like a bad tooth and *a foot out of joint.* Proverbs 25:19 (Italics added)

Broken Hand

The hand is the servant of the body. The hand is used to feed the body. When the hand is broken, you become dysfunctional and your ability to effectively serve is handicapped. God uses His hand to serve the Body of Christ as is evidenced in the following:

"And He Himself gave some to be apostles, some prophets, some evangelists, and some pastors and teachers, for the equipping of the saints for the work of ministry, for the edifying of the body of Christ..." Ephesians 4:11-12

In Ephesians we see God's hand functioning – the Apostles as being the thumb; the index finger being the prophet; the middle finger being the evangelist; the ring finger being that of the pastor and the little finger being the teacher.

The hand also speaks of fellowship:

"...and when James, Cephas, and John, who seemed to be pillars, perceived the grace that had been given to me, they gave me and Barnabas the right hand of fellowship..." Galatians 2:9

When the hand is broken you cannot serve the body and by extension fellowship is broken.

This is why the concept of an "independent church or ministry" has to be incorrect. It gives me the image of someone with a broken hand that has not been restored. They cannot fellowship with anyone and therefore they walk alone declaring "independence". Relationship is the fabric and foundation of the church of Jesus Christ.

Chapter 6 – Part III
Qualifications And
Blemishes Of The Priesthood
III

Hunch-Backed

Hunchback is a non-medical term when there is a forward bending of the spine. The medical term doctors use to describe this condition is called *"kyphosis."* This shape is caused by a condition that deforms the bones of the upper part of the spine so that the person is bent forward causing a hump or an upward arching of the back. The spine, better known as "spinal column" is very important in the body's movement and efficient functioning and it forms the major part of the skeleton. Its importance is recognized as the skull, shoulder bones, ribs, and pelvis are attached to it. A person suffering from this condition looses the ability to carry weight and his/her ability to do great amounts of strenuous physical work is severely hindered, if not at all possible.

Spiritually this represents the believer with no backbone. He is a wimp and cannot take pressure. He is easily swayed or moved. He is not able to keep his hand on the plough with any consistency and is described as one who is not fit for Kingdom use:

> "Then He said to another, "Follow Me." But he said, "Lord, let me first go and bury my father." Jesus said to him, "Let the dead bury their own dead, but you go and preach the kingdom of God." And another also said "Lord, I will follow You, but let me first go and bid them farewell who are at my house." But Jesus said to him, "No one, having put his hand to the plough, and looking back, is fit for the kingdom of God."   Luke 9:59-62

> "Another time, when he invited a man to come with him and to be his disciple, the man agreed-but wanted to wait until his father's death. Jesus replied, "Let those without eternal life concern themselves with things like that. Your duty is to come and preach the coming of the Kingdom of God to all the world." Another said, "Yes, Lord, I will come, but first let me ask permission of those at home." But Jesus told him, "*Anyone who lets himself be distracted from the work I plan for him is not fit for the Kingdom of God.*"   Luke 9:59-62 (Italics added) *TLB*

If one is "*spiritually hunchbacked*" that person should not be leading God's people.

The Dwarf

This is a genetic condition resulting in a short stature and is identified as the process of aging without the corresponding growth.   While this condition in the natural realm will not disqualify a New Testament believer from fulfilling his or her priestly function it will most certainly do, if that person is *"spiritually dwarfed"*.

The Lord wants His people to grow into the fullness of the measure of the stature of Christ and He will not send someone that is *"spiritually dwarfed"* to accomplish this.

The scripture declares:

"And *He Himself gave* some to be *apostles*, some *prophets*, some *evangelists*, and some *pastors* and *teachers*, for the equipping of the saints for the work of ministry, for the edifying of the body of Christ, *till we all come to* the unity of the faith and of the knowledge of the Son of God, to a perfect man, to *the measure of the stature of the fullness of Christ…"* Ephesians 4:11-14 (Italics added)

There is a pre-determined stature we are to arrive at – it is Christ and He was not *"spiritually dwarfed"*.   All the heroes of the faith were men and women of *"full stature"* – who accomplished great exploits for the Lord and we in this hour cannot be anything less as we step into the climax of the ages.

Blemish In The Eye
A blemish in the eye is quite different from being blind; this happens when a person's sight is impaired thereby impeding their visual ability. For example, a person with cataract or colour blindness, while that person may not be

necessarily blind, the ailment could seriously hamper their visual perception. In some cases this could be worse than blindness, as erroneous decisions could be made as a result of misconception.

Spiritually this condition could occur when some strange doctrine, attitude or foreign matter goes into the eye and impairs the vision. We will do well to look at Isaiah whose vision of the Lord was impaired because of king Uzziah:

> "In the year that King Uzziah died, I saw the Lord sitting on a throne, high and lifted up, and the train of His robe filled the temple. Above it stood seraphim; each one had six wings: with two he covered his face, with two he covered his feet, and with two he flew. And one cried to another and said: "Holy, holy, holy is the LORD of hosts; The whole earth is full of His glory!" And the posts of the door were shaken by the voice of him who cried out, and the house was filled with smoke. So I said: "Woe is me, for I am undone! Because I am a man of unclean lips, And I dwell in the midst of a people of unclean lips; For my eyes have seen the King, The LORD of hosts." Then one of the seraphim flew to me, having in his hand a live coal which he had taken with the tongs from the altar. And he touched my mouth with it, and said: "Behold, this has touched your lips; Your iniquity is taken away, And your sin purged." Also I heard the voice of the Lord, saying: "Whom shall I send, And who will go for Us?" Then I said, "Here am I! Send me." Isaiah 6:1-8

In the preceding passage Isaiah's vision was blurred by his vision of king Uzziah. King Uzziah can represent anything that we value more than the Lord and that which is impeding our sight. It was only when king Uzziah died that Isaiah saw the Lord and his true condition. If there is a blemish in the eye one is disqualified from effective service. We need clear vision to flow with God in these end-times.

The scripture further goes on to declare:

"And why do you look at the speck in your brother's eye, but do not consider the plank in your own eye? Or how can you say to your brother, 'Let me remove the speck from your eye'; and look, a plank is in your own eye? Hypocrite! First remove the plank from your own eye, and then you will see clearly to remove the speck out of your brother's eye. Matthew 7:3-5

A blemish in the eye causes inaccurate perception and the Lord strictly warns that one should never attempt to bring correction or adjustment in that condition.

Scurvy - Eczema Or Skin Disease

This is a disease in human beings caused by a prolonged deficiency of vitamin C, or ascorbic acid, in the diet. It is characterized by progressive bodily weakness, spongy and inflamed gums, loose teeth, swollen and tender joints, and a tendency toward ecchymosis, or absorption by the tissues of blood from ruptured blood vessels. Anemia often occurs as a direct result of such hemorrhage. A lack of vitamin C intake results in the absorption and decreased production by the body of the intercellular material that supports the fibrous tissues and forms the cement substance of capillaries, bone, dentin, and cartilage. The disease may appear in adults after about six months of complete lack of vitamin C. Scurvy became prevalent when sailors began to spend months at sea without fresh vegetables, and in such cases it was usually fatal.[88]

Sad to say but quite a number of believers have been living on *"canned sermons"* and as such find themselves suffering from *"spiritual scurvy"* and never being able to step into the higher things in God. They find themselves falling into the category of saints spoken of in Hebrews:

> "For though by this time you ought to be teachers, you need someone to teach you again the first principles of the oracles of God; and you have come to need milk and not solid food. For everyone who partakes only of milk is unskilled in the word of righteousness, for he is a babe. But solid food belongs to those who are of full age, that is, those who by reason of use have their senses exercised to discern both good and evil." Hebrews 5:12-14

They also qualify to fall into the other category of:

> "Having a form of godliness but denying its power. And from such people turn away! For of this sort are those who creep into households and make captives of gullible women loaded down with sins, led away by

---

[88] [88]"Scurvy," *Microsoft® Encarta® Encyclopedia 2000.*

various lusts, always learning and never able to come to the knowledge of the truth." 2 Timothy 3:5-7

A congregation that feeds only on *"canned sermons"* will produce *"Itchers"* who will not be able to endure sound doctrine and after a while they will fulfill the word spoken by the Apostle Paul to Timothy:

> "Preach the word! Be ready in season and out of season. Convince, rebuke, exhort, with all longsuffering and teaching. For the time will come when they will not endure sound doctrine, but according to their own desires, because they have itching ears, they will heap up for themselves teachers; and they will turn their ears away from the truth, and be turned aside to fables. 2 Timothy 4:2-5

In order to fully function in our king/priest anointing we must continue having a fresh supply of God's revelation truth ministered to and from our hearts – we must continue in "present truth". We must have a regular diet of "fresh food" similar to what the Israelites had in their journey to the Promised Land; it must be fresh and not stale as they were not to live on "canned or preserved" food:

> "This is the thing which the LORD has commanded: 'Let every man gather it according to each one's need, one omer for each person, according to the number of persons; let every man take for those who are in his tent.' "And the children of Israel did so and gathered, some more, some less. So when they measured it by

omers, he who gathered much had nothing over, and he who gathered little had no lack. Every man had gathered according to each one's need. And Moses said, "*Let no one leave any of it till morning.*" Notwithstanding they did not heed Moses. *But some of them left part of it until morning, and it bred worms and stank.* And Moses was angry with them. So they gathered it every morning, every man according to his need. And when the sun became hot, it melted." Exodus 16:16-21 (Italics added)

The New Testament priest of God must be able to minister the current word from God. He/she must be in tune with what the Spirit is saying to the Church today. The people of God should not feed on canned sermons and left over manna, but instead, if we are to be all that God intended and to bring the Church into the fullness of the measure of the stature of Jesus Christ we must supply Her with a rich diet full of fresh truth from God's Holy Spirit.

Scabs

A scab is the covering that is formed over a wound that has not yet healed. It is very different from a scar, which is a mark left after a wound is healed. As you would notice, scripture disqualified anyone who had a scab from ministering, and did not mention anything about scars. However, as they can look very similar, there is a way you can tell the difference. When pressure is applied to the spot – the scar will withstand it, but the scab will produce pain, and at times even break open and release an odorous substance called pus.

Spiritually speaking, a scab is the result of a wound that is not healed. Please understand that in this walk we will be wounded – we are in a war against a sinister enemy called the devil – however, the Lord has made every provision for us to be completely healed if we ever were to be wounded. Scabs in the believer's life are caused by unforgiveness. When we forgive, wounds are turned into scars of victory, but when we don't, they turn into scabs of torment. The best example we have of this is Jesus, as He was paying the ultimate price for your sins and mine and the entire world. This is what He said:

> "And when they had come to the place called Calvary, there they crucified Him, and the criminals, one on the right hand and the other on the left. Then Jesus said, *"Father, forgive them*, for they do not know what they do."'" Luke 23:33-34 (Italics added)

What an incredible event! What an awesome example! Jesus is the prime example of the power of forgiveness. He carries in His Body scars of the battle and not scabs from unhealed wounds. Thomas understood this and wanted to make sure it was Jesus and declared that he would not believe unless he examined the wounds for himself:

> "Now Thomas, called the Twin, one of the twelve, was not with them when Jesus came. The other disciples therefore said to him, "We have seen the Lord. "*So he said to them, "Unless I see in His hands the print of the nails, and put my finger into the print of the nails, and put my hand into His side, I will not believe."* And after

eight days His disciples were again inside, and Thomas
with them. *Jesus came*, the doors being shut, and stood
in the midst, and said, "Peace to you! "*Then He said to
Thomas, "Reach your finger here, and look at My
hands; and reach your hand here, and put it into My
side*. Do not be unbelieving, but believing." And
Thomas answered and said to Him, "My Lord and my
God!"" John 20:24-28 (Italics added)

Hallelujah! Glory to God! The scars are still there
because of forgiveness. When we do not forgive we retain
the injury and go through torment. We remain with
wounds covered with scabs and as soon as pressure is
applied, they break open.

Sometimes you hear men and women of God rake up
old hurts and pains, signifying bondage to the incident and
the offender. Instead of carrying in their body the example
set by Jesus in His death; they carry the hurt and pain of an
unhealed wound.

The Word of God declares that when we do not forgive
we walk in torment:

"Then Peter came to Him and said, "Lord, *how often
shall my brother sin against me, and I forgive him*? Up
to seven times?" Jesus said to him, "I do not say to
you, up to seven times, but up to seventy times seven.
Therefore the kingdom of heaven is like a certain king
who wanted to settle accounts with his servants. And
when he had begun to settle accounts, one was brought
to him who owed him ten thousand talents. But as he

was not able to pay, his master commanded that he be sold, with his wife and children and all that he had, and that payment be made. The servant therefore fell down before him, saying, 'Master have patience with me, and I will pay you all.' "Then the master of that servant was moved with compassion, released him, and forgave him the debt. But that servant went out and found one of his fellow servants who owed him a hundred denarii; and he laid hands on him and took him by the throat, saying, 'Pay me what you owe!' "So his fellow servant fell down at his feet and begged him, saying, 'Have patience with me, and I will pay you all.' "And he would not, but went and threw him into prison till he should pay the debt. So when his fellow servants saw what had been done, they were very grieved, and came and told their master all that had been done. Then his master, after he had called him, said to him, 'You wicked servant! I forgave you all that debt because you begged me. Should you not also have had compassion on your fellow servant, just as I had pity on you?' "And his master was angry, and *delivered him to the torturers* until he should pay all that was due to him. *So My heavenly Father also will do to you if each of you, from his heart, does not forgive his brother his trespasses.*" Matthew 18:21-35 (Italics added)

As the Lord brings His Church into greater dimensions of function in these last days, there is a greater demand from His Spirit for us to walk in these *levels of purity*. We must forgive if we are to minister the true life of God to others. We cannot afford to minister the life of God to others from a wounded or critical spirit.

If, as you read through the pages of this book, and you know that you are at odds against anyone, I urge you to make it right in your heart this very moment. Stop reading and call on your heavenly Father and release the hurt, release the person who has wronged you now; do not walk with the injury and pain any longer, this is your moment of release. You are called to be a king/priest unto God and to deal the Bread of God to the hungry, but you will be disqualified if you do not forgive and release others.

Broken Stones

In the Hebrew, the word for "stones" is the word "Eshek" which is rendered *testicles*. This is the male reproductive organ. One of the qualifications of the Old Testament priest was that he had fully functioning reproductive organs. This was so that he could assist in keeping the lineage of the priesthood. The Lord also laid down very [89]strict regulations as to who they were to marry in His desire to keep the priesthood pure.

In like manner God requires the New Testament royal priest to have his "spiritual testicles" fully functioning. This is why the full release and function of the Apostles are so vital in this hour. God is releasing through the apostolic true [90]fathers who are bringing forth Christ in His people. Not just husbands – (representing "pastors" who are *"married"* to the flock and can do the all-important task of shepherding, tending and taking care of their needs) but

---

[89] Leviticus 21:7,13-14
[90] You can read the author's book "Five Pillars of The Apostolic" for a more in-depth analysis on true Fathering.

but fathers – (representing "Apostles" who have been graced by God with a *"fathering anointing"* to reproduce or form Christ in the sheep). The Apostle Paul declared this:

> "I do not write these things to shame you, but as my beloved children I warn you. For though you might have ten thousand *instructors* in Christ, *yet you do not have many fathers*; for in Christ Jesus I have begotten you through the gospel." 1 Corinthians 4:14-15 (Italics added)

> "My little children, for whom I *labour in birth* again until Christ is formed in you…" Galatians 4:19 (Italics added)

Please understand that excellent ministry is not fulfilled until it reproduces!

Jesus told His Apostles before He returned to the Father that they were to go and make disciples (*not just converts*).

He declared:
> "And Jesus came and spoke to them, saying, "All authority has been given to Me in heaven and on earth. Go therefore and *make disciples* of all the nations, baptizing them in the name of the Father and of the Son and of the Holy Spirit, *teaching them* to observe all things that I have commanded you; and lo, I am with you always, even to the end of the age." Amen." Matthew 28:18-20 (Italics added)

Jesus imparted His life into these men and now He was

commanding them to do the same. God is after quality reproduction. Everything brings forth after its own kind, so in order for us to reproduce powerful, strong ministry in this end-time we must be pure and only then will we reproduce right.

We are the by-products of what we receive – we are shaped by the revelation that is spoken to us; Jesus said:

"Man shall not live by bread alone, but by every word that proceeds from the mouth of God." Matthew 4:4

He also declared in John 6:63:

"It is the Spirit who gives life; the flesh profits nothing. The words that I speak to you are spirit, and they are life."

By extension, the Church of Jesus Christ is being built upon the revelation that God is releasing through His ordained government. This is why it is so important for ministry to flow out of pure hearts. Again we can draw from Jesus as He spoke to His disciples in the book of John:

"I am the true vine, and My Father is the vinedresser. Every branch in Me that does not bear fruit He takes away; and every branch that bears fruit He prunes, that it may bear more fruit. *You are already clean because of the word which I have spoken to you… If you abide in Me, and My words abide in you*, you will ask what you desire, and it shall be done for you. By this *My*

Father is glorified, that you bear much fruit; so you will be My disciples." John 15:1-3, 7-8 (Italics added)

Jesus was teaching the process of true *"spiritual reproduction"* – He spoke the word of God to His disciples out of a pure heart and He declared to them that they were clean because of the word that He ministered to them. He goes on to instruct them that they will only reproduce if they first become like Him and allow His words to live in them.

In all that we do, our emphasis must be on *becoming* like Christ. If we only concentrate on the *"doing"* without the *"becoming"* we will be accorded an unpleasant surprise on "awards night". – It will be extremely sad to hear Jesus say, "I never knew you; depart from Me."[91]

However, disqualification does not have to be a permanent feature of your life if you find yourself suffering from one or more of the aforementioned spiritual conditions.

In Leviticus we read the following:

"No man of the descendants of Aaron the priest, who has a defect, shall come near to offer the offerings made by fire to the LORD. He has a defect; he shall not come near to offer the bread of his God. *He may eat the bread of his God, both the most holy and the holy…*"   Leviticus 21:21-22 (Italics added)

---

[91] Matthew 7:23

Praise God! The word of God declares that anyone called to be a priest that has a defect although he must not deal the Bread of God to the people he can eat the Bread both of the holy and the most holy. Leadership is a critical issue in the present move of God's Spirit and issues of purity must begin at the head. God wants His leaders to be of a *high calibre*, because everything rises and falls on leadership.

If you are reading this book and you are in leadership and have one of these spiritual defects that has not be healed and delivered, this is the time for you to allow the Holy Spirit to deal with it.

I declare to you by the Spirit of the living God, that this is the hour to cast aside every weight and to cast down every high thing that is seeking to exalt itself against the knowledge and revelation of Christ in your life. Now is the time to press into the Lord. Now is the time to hunger and thirst after righteousness. There is a greater demand from the Spirit of the Lord in these days as He restores His apostles back into the Church. I urge you at this point to establish covenants of obedience with the Lord – declare to Him "Lord, I covenant with You that I will be obedient to Your word. Lord, You command me and I will obey You."

There is so much more that can be written in a book of this nature, however, it is my prayer that the chapters of this book will be a tremendous source of strength and encouragement to all who read them. That you will be driven in pursuit of *His Excellence*, remembering the words of the Apostle Peter:

> "Therefore gird up the loins of your mind, be sober, and rest your hope fully upon the grace that is to be brought to you at the revelation of Jesus Christ; as obedient children, not conforming yourselves to the former lusts, as in your ignorance; but as He who called you is holy, you also be holy in all your conduct, because it is written, "Be holy, for I am holy." 1 Peter 1:13-16

Appendix
Apostolic Definition/Reference In Scripture

In the Strong's Concordance the word "Apostle" is rendered "Apostolos" (ap-os-tol-oss) in the Greek, and conveys the following meaning: "A special messenger, a delegate, one commissioned for a particular task or role, one who is sent forth with a message. One who is sent to represent another in the power and authority of the one who sent him." In the final analysis, that person is similar to that of an ambassador.[92]

When God calls one to be an Apostle, He releases His power and authority upon that individual, commissions and sends that person to function.

When the Church was being established, it was done upon the foundation laid by the Apostles and Prophets[93]. Most people believe that the death of the early Apostles and Prophets meant that it was the end of Apostles and Prophets in the body of Christ. However, a thorough search of the scriptures establishes the fact, that there were more Apostles than the original twelve. For a brief look we can cite the following scriptures:

"Moreover, brethren, I declare to you that the gospel which I preached to you, which also you received and in which you stand, by which also you are saved, if you hold fast that word which I preached to you – unless

---

[92] For more on present-day apostles, see the author's book "Five Pillars of The Apostolic"

[93] Ephesians 2:20

you believed in vain. For I delivered to you first of all that which I also received; that Christ died for our sins according to the scriptures, And that He was buried, and that He rose again the third day according to the Scriptures, And that He was seen by Cephas, *then by the twelve* [that is the original twelve Apostles]. After that He was seen by over five hundred brethren at once, of whom the greater part remain to the present, but some have fallen asleep. After that He was seen by James, *then by all the Apostles* (I submit to you that this was referring to the other Apostles, apart from the original twelve). Then last of all He was seen by me also, as by one born out of due time." 1 Corinthians 15:1–8 (Italics and Parenthesis added)

'The Twelve' is a regular designation of the Apostles in the Gospels, and Paul uses it in 1 Corinthians 15:5. Its symbolic appropriateness is obvious, and recurs in such places as Revelation 21:14. The whole Matthias incident in Acts 1:15-26 is concerned with making up the number of the Twelve. Yet Paul's consciousness of Apostleship is equally clear (1 Corinthians 1:1; 2 Corinthians 1:1; Galatians 1:1; Ephesians 1:1; Colossians 1:1; 1 Timothy 1:1; 2 Timothy 1:1; Titus 1:1). Further, there are instances in the New Testament where, others outside the Twelve are given the title. James the Lord's brother in Galatians 1:19; 2:9, and, though he was not a disciple (John 7:5), received a resurrection appearance personal to himself (1 Corinthians 15:7). Barnabas is called an Apostle in Acts 14:4, 14, and is introduced by Paul into an argument that denies any qualitative difference between his own Apostleship and that of the Twelve (1 Corinthians 9:1-6).

The unknown Andronicus and Junias are called Apostles in Romans 16:7. Again in 1 Thessalonians 1:1; 2:6 Paul, describes Silvanus, Timothy and himself as Apostles.

Other Titles By The Author

Five Pillars Of The Apostolic

Towards A Mature Church

D iscerning seasons and times is such an important task in the day that we live. If, as the body of the LORD we fail to do so, we will fail in expressing the heart of Father God. It has become very evident that a new day has dawned in the earth, as the Lord restores the foundational ministry of the Apostle back to His Church. There is an awesome, powerful, militant church rising in the earth, as Apostles are being restored to take their place alongside the Prophets, Evangelists, Pastors and Teachers to bring the Church into unity and to a place of maturity for function in the earth. It is indeed a glorious time to be alive and be connected to the purpose of the Lord.

The body of Christ truly is reaching unprecedented levels of power, revelation, and effectiveness. Michael Scantlebury is a keen observer of this historic transition and the key role that apostles are playing in it. Five Pillars of the Apostolic has my recommendation. **C. Peter Wagner, Chancellor,** Wagner Leadership Institute

The 21st century has exploded in Apostolic revelation and understanding... I highly recommend this book not only to church leaders but to lay people everywhere... **Apostle Emanuele Cannistraci** Apostolic Leader of Apostolic Missions International San Jose, California, USA

This book provides an excellent tool for the Church to measure apostolic claims by the yardstick of the author's five-pillars of apostolic grace... **Dr. Roger W. Sapp** All Nations Ministries Southlake, Texas, USA

Rooted firmly in biblical teachings this book is a "must" for all leaders who desire to keep their Churches on the cutting edge... **Pastor Ajith Abeyratne** Senior Pastor, Calvary Church Mirihana, Sri Lanka

Kingdom Advancing Prayer
Volumes I & II

Part of the technology that is being released into the Church as the Lord restores Apostles, is what we describe as Kingdom Advancing Prayer. This kind of prayer puts the Kingdom of God first and foremost; it is above any personal need or agenda. It is similar to the kind of prayer that Elijah prayed, as the Lord used him to turn a whole nation around, and destroy the demonic influence that threatened to thwart the Lord's purpose. It is reflective of the prayer that Jesus prayed as He prepared to bring to completion His Father's will and go to the cross.

The Church of Jesus Christ is stronger and much more determined and equipped than she has ever been, and strong, aggressive, powerful, Spirit-Filled, Kingdom-centred prayers are being lifted in every nation in the earth. We are seeing the emergence of Houses of Prayer all over the earth with prayer going up 24/7. Prayer is calling for the Bridegroom's return, and for the Bride to be made ready. Prayers that are storming the heavens and binding the "strong men", declaring and decreeing God's Kingdom rule in every jurisdiction. This is what we call Kingdom Advancing Prayer. This kind of prayer is released from the heart of Father God into the hearts of His people, as we seek for His Glory to cover the earth as the waters cover the sea. What a GLORIOUS DAY to be ALIVE and to be in the WILL and PLAN of FATHER GOD! HALLELUJAH!

To Order Contact:
Word Alive Press Inc.
131 Cordite Road · Winnipeg, MB, R3W 1S1 · Canada
Phone: 866.967.3782 · Fax: 800.352.9272

Identifying And Defeating The Jezebel Spirit

I declare to you with the greatest of conviction that we are living in the days when Malachi 4:5-6 is being fulfilled. The Elijah spirit is truly in the earth as the Lord prepares His Church for the return of Jesus and the culmination of all things. However, as it was in the days of Elijah of old so it is in these days.

Elijah in his day had to confront and deal with a false spiritual order and government that was established and set up by an evil woman called Jezebel and her spineless husband called Ahab. This spirit is still active in the earth and in the Church; however the Lord is restoring His holy apostles and prophets to identify and destroy this spirit as recorded in Revelation 2:18-23

As you read through the pages of this book it is my prayer that you will be enlightened to the reality of the battle and the strategy the Lord has given us to effect the ultimate victory.

To Order Contact:
Dominion-Life International
Box 44592 Garden Park, PO
Vancouver, BC, V5M 4R8, Canada
Phone: 604-953-1087 · Fax: 604-293-7751
Or visit our website at http://www.dominion-life.org

Other Titles Recommended By The Author

Authored By Dr. **Kelley Varner**

Moses, the Master and the Manchild ISBN 0-7684-2121-7

The Three Prejudices   ISBN 1-56043-187-3

The More Excellent Ministry   ISBN 0-914903-60-8

The Priesthood is Changing   ISBN 1-56043-033-8

Prevail   ISND 0-938612-06-9

To Order Contact Destiny Image
P.O. Box 310, Shippensburg, PA 17257-0310
Or on the Internet at
www.reapernet.com

Authored By **Apostle John Eckhardt**

Moving in the Apostolic   ISBN 0-8307-2373-0

The Ministry Anointing   ISBN 0-9630567-6-X
Of The Apostle

Leadershift – Transitioning from ISBN 1-883927-14-5
the Pastoral to the Apostolic

Presbyteries and Apostolic Teams ISBN 1-883927-13-7

Proton Believers   ISBN 1-883927-15-3

50 Truths Concerning   ISBN 1-883927-04-8
Apostolic Ministry

To Order Contact Crusaders I.M.P.A.C.T
P.O. Box 492, Matteson, IL 60443
708-922-0983
www.impactnetwork.net

Authored By **Dr. Jonathan David**

Apostolic Strategies Affecting Nations

Proclaiming Liberty To The Captives

Developing A Prophetic Ministry

Business Sense For Making Dollars

Jesus, God's Greatest Move

To Order Contact Crusaders I.M.P.A.C.T
P.O. Box 492, Matteson, IL 60443
708-922-0983
www.impactnetwork.net

OR

Dr. Jonathan David
No: 4, Taman Mas Ria, Jalan Junid,
84000 Muar, Jahor Malaysia
Tel: (06)-9534066 Fax: (06)-9531031
www.jonathan-david.org

Authored By **Dr. Noel Woodroffe**

The Present Reformation	ISBN 976-8115-03-3
The Prophetic Dimension	ISBN 976-8115-05-X
Spiritual Government	ISBN 976-8115-00-9
The Ultimate Warrior	ISBN 976-8115-01-7

To Order Contact Elijah Centre
P.O. Bag 317, Tunapuna, Trinidad, W.I
Phone 868-662-5673
www.elijahcentre.org

Authored By **Dr. Roger Sapp**

The Last Apostles on Earth   ISBN 1-56043-568-2

Apostolic Fathers and   ISBN 0-9662085-4-4
Spiritual Bastards

Performing Miracles and Healing   ISBN 0-9662085-5-2

To Order Contact All Nations Ministry
P.O. Box 92847, Southlake, TX 76092
817-514-0653
www.allnationsmin.org

Authored By **Pastor Jana Alcorn**

The Ministry of Excellence

Prophetic Encounters--Facilitating Change Through the Voice
of the Spirit

To Order Contact Harvest Church
700 Motley Street - PO Box 205
Albertville, Alabama 35950
Phone 256-891-1650
www.MinistryOfExcellence.com

Authored By **Symon Boschma**

The Coming Days of Thunder   ISBN 1579212263

To Order Contact Winepress Publishing
P. O. Box 1046, Mukilteo, WA 98275 USA
Phone 800-917-2665

Printed in the United States
36272LVS00002B/85